LOUIS NOWRA was born in Melbourne. He is the author of such plays as *Inner Voices, Visions, Inside the Island, The Precious Woman, Sunrise, The Golden Age, Capricornia, Byzantine Flowers, The Watchtower, Summer of the Aliens, Cosi, Radiance, The Temple, Crow, Miss Bosnia, The Incorruptible, The Jungle* and *The Language of the Gods.* He has written a non-fiction work *The Cheated,* three novels *The Miser of Beauty, Palu, Red Nights* and a memoir *The Twelfth of Never.* Some of his radio plays include *Albert Names Edward, The Song Room, The Widows, Sydney* and *Moon of the Exploding Trees.* Besides translating such plays as *The Prince of Homburg, Cyrano de Bergerac* and *Lulu,* he has written the libretti for *Whitsunday* and *Love Burns.* Telemovies are *Displaced Persons, Hunger* and *The Lizard King.* He wrote the screenplays for *Map of the Human Heart, Cosi, Heaven's Burning* and *Radiance.* He lives in Sydney.

ABOUT LOUIS NOWRA

Veronica Kelly, *The Theatre of Louis Nowra*
This highly illuminating book about the life and work of Louis Nowra is an important contribution to our understanding of one of Australia's major writers. The author, Dr Veronica Kelly, is a lecturer in the English Department of the University of Queensland.

SUMMER
OF THE
ALIENS

LOUIS NOWRA

Currency Press • Sydney

First published in 1992 by
Currency Press Pty Ltd
PO Box 2287, Strawberry Hills, NSW 2012
www.currency.com.au,
enquiries@currency.com.au

Reprinted 1994, 1996, 1998, 2000, 2002, 2004, 2007, 2010, 2012

NATIONAL LIBRARY OF AUSTRALIA
Nowra, Louis, 1950–.
    Summer of the Aliens
    ISBN 978 0 86819 325 0
    1. Title.
    A822.3

Cover design by Trevor Hood
Printed by Griffin Press, Adelaide

Contents

I was a Teenage Alien

Louis Nowra

The past makes our present. We can never escape from the past
no matter how far we want to run. It can be said that it's not so
much that we can't go home again, but that we have never left
home. One of the themes of *Summer of the Aliens* is that the
past has made the narrator what he is – no matter how much the
older Lewis has changed there is still a connection to his
younger self. But if there are differences, and there are, one of
the main ones is that the older Lewis in growing up has, like all
adults, left behind a major part of his childhood, or, for want of
a better word, a part of his soul.

This play is a black hole of fiction, surrounded by a halo of
truth. It has many autobiographical elements and although there
are many factual and chronological discrepencies, I have tried
to keep true to the emotional chronology of my youth. This is
a chronology that can place the Cuban crisis in summer, when
it was, in fact, earlier and place the curious behaviour of
someone like Pisano in a shorter space of time than it was in
reality. Memory is remembered emotion, not facts. In my mind
the Cuban crisis did occur around the time of my obsession with
flying saucers and aliens.

Why is this so, I ask myself? One of the reasons must be the
science fiction films of the fifties and early sixties. In such films
as *I Married a Monster from Outer Space, It Conquered the
World* and *Invasion of the Body Snatchers*, it is easy to see that
the aliens who came to conquer earth were not unlike the

Communists who threatened to destroy us (that is, western democracies). To people like myself and many Australians, young and old, the Russians were as foreign, as potentially evil as any alien. It is obvious then how I could conflate the Cuban crisis with my fascination for UFOs.

This interest in flying saucers was fueled by two events. One night I saw a television interview with a George Adamski who talked of how he had been abducted by Venusians and they had taken him to Venus where 'I ate apples just like on earth'. He was delivered back to earth where they informed him that aliens walked amongst humans, pretending to be like us, so that they could examine and learn about us. This idea that aliens could seem like humans scared me, as did the film *Invaders from Mars*, where a boy discovers that his parents are not his true parents but aliens who have taken over their bodies. Again both events instilled in me the awful realisation that it was not possible to be certain about the humanity of people, or more insidiously, the humanity of your own parents, your own flesh and blood. No doubt, my own uncertainty about what it meant to be an adult, about growing from a boy into a man and my uncertainty about my sexuality played an enormous part in all of this.

The landscape of the play is recognisably Fawkner, a suburb to the north of Melbourne. For years the only thing notable about it was that it housed the dead. Fawkner cemetery was the only thing that grew. The rest of the suburb was paddocks. There were very few trees, only long grass, cracked earth and the only colour was the purple scotch thistles in spring. In 1949 the Housing Commission built 113 houses. The experiment proved a public relations disaster. The houses, constructed out of concrete blocks, may have been cheap but they had no sewerage and the roads were unmade (it was not until 1960 that the Housing Commission attempted to build again in Fawkner). My family lived in one of these 113 houses, in a landscape so drab and boring that only the landscape of the mind offered colour and excitement.

To the north-west of Fawkner was the suburb of Broadmeadows, again a landscape filled with the featureless volcanic plains of paddocks, from which our school took in pupils, many of them immigrants from Europe, especially England and the Netherlands. Surprisingly although there was a dislike of these immigrants, the greatest hatred was directed towards the pommies. I think the reason for this was so many of us, who belonged to the working class, were of Irish or Scottish descent and therefore had the collective memory of our ancestors and even our parent's dislike of English imperialism. I vividly remember a pommy arriving in our class one summer (and it's curious, but I do not remember winter in my childhood) and you could see in his scared eyes, that he knew he had better act tough. Someone asked him his name and he said 'Rocky'. We all laughed because he was so short and wan looking. At lunch we took him out to play cricket. He said he could bat. I opened the bowling and after one ball I could see he was woeful at the game. In our neighbourhood you seldom took pity on the weak, so the next ball was a bouncer. He turned when he saw it coming, as if he wanted to run away and it hit him on the back. Everyone jeered. He was just a pathetic pommy after all.

When, in my early teenage years, our family shifted to a middle class suburb, my mother took the stunted trees and shrubs which had not grown in the Fawkner soil and planted them in the rich, loamy soil of Macleod. Within a year they had doubled their size. The metaphor was obvious. Fawkner was barren and sterile, Macleod, fertile and green. My own development was different. I took with me the values and attitudes of Fawkner only to discover quickly that my brashness and aggression were seen by my new middle class neighbours, school mates and teachers as the behaviour of an insensitive yobbo. In order to survive the hardest training ground in the world – the school yard – I quickly tried to change myself. So deliberate was this attempt at transformation that I would copy the gestures and vocal mannerisms of boys I particularly admired in order to be like them, sometimes uncannily like them. In a way it was like an alien studying a new world, trying to mimic and ape the inhabitants of his new world as closely as possible.

Working class life is lived at a much shriller level. Violence and aggression are not sublimated into manners and patterns of decorum. In *Summer of the Aliens* I have tried to feature this and the quickness with which people react to imagined slights or differences. It was a world where the arrival of a policeman was a tense stand off, where neighbours had criminal records, where theatre and art were regarded as a poofter activity and where to survive and be part of your group you had to be seen to be tough and resilient. Sometimes I imagine, fantasise is probably the right word, how I would have ended up if I had stayed in Fawkner. I see myself as a truckie, with a beer belly and six or seven kids, down at the pub most nights, an ocker guy, enjoying his truck, his booze, his mates and his unambitious life. If anything the late sixties and early seventies shattered one of the essential features of the fifties and early sixties – the preordained nature of the course of your life. There would be school, early marriage, children, attractive suburban home, work in the same job, retirement and death. With the arrival of the seventies came affluence and young people rebelled against this ideal. It seemed possible to escape from this conformity, this preordained pattern to your life (something I play with in *Cosi*, my follow up work to this play).

Originally *Summer of the Aliens* was written for radio. In adapting it for the stage there is a considerable shift in emphasis. The radio play is an impressionistic portrait of the neighbourhood seen through the eyes of a boy who is having trouble understanding the world around him. The stage play centres on relationships, especially the relationship between Lewis and Dulcie. It is through Dulcie that Lewis begins to understand that the struggle to be adult is the struggle to understand the world around him. One of the important words he must understand is the word Dulcie asks him to name ('What is that word, Lewis?'). It is a word I still have trouble understanding. If anything distinguishes the two versions it is the endings. In the radio version Lewis runs away; in the stage play he stays with his family, having, through Dulcie, begun to understand that the people around him are not possessed by aliens but by drives and emotions we label 'human'.

My work is generally not regarded as being autobiographical. Where other playwrights obviously mine the ore of their own lives, until now I have not, although I can see in such plays of mine as *Inner Voices, Inside the Island, The Golden Age* and *Byzantine Flowers*, a hidden, and to me, powerful undercurrent of emotional autobiography. This is not to say that *Summer of the Aliens* is an autobiographical play. It is more a work of fiction with autobiographical elements. I can say that there are aspects of my own parents in Norma and Eric but in reality they were different people, just as I was, though to a lesser degree. What I have done is act like Frankenstein. Like the doctor I have raided the graveyard of my memory and have created a monster out of the various limbs and appendages I could dig up.

Why now? Why haven't I, like a lot of other writers, written autobiographical plays earlier in my career? I have no answer except that now, when I'm drinking in a bar I am beginning to see more often that potbellied truckdriver, with his bog Irish face, swapping stories and lies with his mates. I'm beginning to be less condescending towards him and I'm liking him more and more.

Melbourne, December 1991

Summer of the Aliens was first performed by the Melbourne Theatre Company at the Russell Street Theatre, Melbourne, on 17 March 1992, with the following cast:

NARRATOR	Louis Nowra
LEWIS	Tamblyn Lord
DULCIE	Kylie Belling
MR PISANO / UNCLE RICHARD	Ernie Gray
NORMA	Genevieve Picot
ERIC / MR IRVIN	Robert Grubb
GRANDMA / MRS IRVIN / JAPANESE WOMAN	
	Beverley Phillips
BEV / DUTCH GIRL	Josephine Keen
BRIAN	Vince Colosimo

Director: Nadia Tass
Set Designer: Trinia Parker
Costume Designer: Trina Parker
Lighting Designer: Jamieson Lewis
Lighting Operator: Richard Johnstone
Composer: Phillip Judd
Sound Recording: Kerry Saxby
Stage Manager: Greg Diamantis
Assistant StageManager: Margaret Lloyd

CHARACTERS

NARRATOR, the older Lewis
LEWIS, 14 years old
DULCIE, 14 years old
NORMA, Lewis' mother
ERIC, Lewis' father
UNCLE RICHARD, Lewis' uncle
BEV, Lewis' sister
GRANDMA, Lewis' Grandma
MR IRVIN, Dulcie's step father
MRS IRVIN, Dulcie's mother
BEATRICE, a Dutch girl
MR PISANO, the postman
BRIAN, Lewis' friend
JAPANESE WOMAN

SETTING

A Housing Commission Estate in the paddocks of northern
Melbourne in the early sixties.

The publisher would like to thank the following for permission to
reproduce photographs: p.25 Herald and Weekly Times Ltd; p.61
Trina Parker; p.77 Hills Hoist courtesy Hills Industries Ltd.

ACT ONE

SCENE ONE

It is late morning in a gully near a shooting range, where men are shooting at clay pigeons. LEWIS crouches in the gully as he buttons up his shirt. DULCIE sits on the ground, grimacing as if in agony.

DULCIE: Please. Please.

> [LEWIS pays no attention to her and peers up over the gully.]

Lewis. Please. I did yours.

> [He reluctantly kneels behind her and lifts up the back of her blouse.]

It's so itchy.

> [He begins to peel her back.]

Careful. I want it off in one strip.

LEWIS: Why?

DULCIE: So we can make a Nazi lamp out of it.

> [The NARRATOR, in his late thirties, enters, wearing a suit, a smart country and western shirt and rattleskin boots, looking like a hybrid American/ Australian.]

NARRATOR: This is the end of the road. A Housing Commission Estate, north of Melbourne. The houses were built of concrete slabs and plonked down on these paddocks that stretch all the way to Sydney.

DULCIE: [to LEWIS] Slowly.

LEWIS: You know, this gully would make a good trench.

DULCIE: What for?

LEWIS: When the communists come. Mum said we'll have to live five to a room then.

DULCIE: Don't talk. Just concentrate on my skin.

NARRATOR: It's just paddocks. Flat all the way to the horizon. There are no trees or flowers, just dry grass and scotch thistles. In summer the earth cracks, in winter it becomes like black clag. Some people have got soil from the Merri Creek to put on their lawns. You can tell their gardens: their flowers and bushes actually grow.

DULCIE: I put tons of butter on it.

LEWIS: Never helps. Cold tea. Vinegar. [Noticing a red mark around her waist.] What's that mark?

DULCIE: Mum said if I tied a rope around my waist that every time I thought impure thoughts I'd tie it tighter so I'd only have the pain to think about. Like the girls of Fatima.

LEWIS: I thought it was because you were practising the hula hoop a lot. [Referring to her skin.] Almost there.

NARRATOR: That's me: Lewis. And that's Dulcie, my friend from a few doors up. We live in Singapore Street. All the streets in our estate are named after famous battles: Gallipoli, Tobruk, Somme, Kokoda, Singapore. [More shots ring out.] Behind the estate is the shooting range. I went there to collect the brass casings from the spent cartridges. I'm waiting in the gully for the shooters to finish.

LEWIS: Do you think there's life on other planets? Damn!

DULCIE: [referring to skin] Oh, no. You broke it!

NARRATOR: The Time. 1962. Summer. A time when people feared that there was going to be a war between Russia and America. A time when we had beaten the West Indian cricket team. It was the year I developed an obsession with flying saucers.

LEWIS: [peering over gully] Hey, he got one. Blind luck. [Recognising one of the shooters] It's Brian's dad. [DULCIE stands to take a look. He pulls her down.] Get down! They'll blow your head off. I don't know why I bothered to take you along.

DULCIE: Get lost.

LEWIS: He must be out of jail.

DULCIE: He owes Stan money. They had some scheme going with a cop, stripping cars.

LEWIS: Maybe he's practising to kill your father.

DULCIE: I'd pay him if he did.

LEWIS: When they passed the dark side of the moon they gave him apples to eat.

DULCIE: Who?

LEWIS: The one I was telling you about. Aliens kidnapped him.

DULCIE: Aliens?

LEWIS: He was on the news. They interviewed him. He said they had apples like ours. Except crispier.

DULCIE: [amused] Kidnapped by aliens.

LEWIS: He was. [They duck as shots ring uncomfortably close.] Brian's dad isn't a good shot. [A beat.] He was taken to Venus. To a gigantic city. He said it was a bit like New York. Only men and women were of the same sex.

DULCIE: How do you tell them apart?

LEWIS: [flummoxed] Don't know. I guess they do.

DULCIE: How do they breed?

LEWIS: Didn't say. [A beat.] It was only a quick trip. Maybe they'll tell him next time.

DULCIE: Why did they kidnap him?

LEWIS: To show him. They said they might come to earth and live with us. They'd run out of water.

DULCIE: Why would they come here, we've got a drought?

LEWIS: [irritated] I don't know. [Peering over the edge] They're going. Let's get the shells.

   [They crawl out of the gully, LEWIS, in his eagerness, rushing ahead. DULCIE stops.]

DULCIE: Lewis!

   [He turns around.]

   Geronimo!

LEWIS: [knowing what is about to happen.] No!

   [She rushes at him and wrestles him to the ground. He gives in and she sits on him.]

DULCIE: You give in too quickly. Fight me.

LEWIS: I don't want to

DULCIE: Wrestle.

LEWIS: Get off.

DULCIE: Fight me.

LEWIS: The scrap merchants close at noon. If I don't get to them in time we won't have the money to go to the pictures.

DULCIE: [reluctantly] All right. [A beat.] Does it feel good?

LEWIS: What?

DULCIE: Me sitting on you.

LEWIS: You're heavy.

DULCIE: Thanks a lot.

　　　　[She gets off him and he jumps up. They start to collect brass casings. LEWIS finds a clay pigeon.]

LEWIS: I bet the flying saucers look like these clay pigeons.

DULCIE: Black?

LEWIS: No, they'd be shinier, like the colour of brass.

　　　　[DULCIE throws the brass she has collected at LEWIS.] What's that for?

DULCIE: I'm not a cripple or something, you don't have to take me to the pictures.

　　　　[MR PISANO, the postman, appears.]

PISANO: Morning, Lewis. Dulcie.

LEWIS: You coming to shoot, Mr Pisano?

PISANO: Taking a short cut through the rifle range. It takes minutes off my round.

DULCIE: Where's your bike?

PISANO: Someone nicked it. Which is typical of this neighbourhood. Anyway, my feet are more reliable, they don't get punctures. [Remembering something before setting off] I told your dad, Lewis, before he pissed off, to paint your number bigger. You do it, you're the man of the house. [To DULCIE] And make your letter box number bigger too.

DULCIE: But you already know it.

PISANO: Listen, girlie, no cheek. Just get the number bigger.

　　　　[He hurries off.]

LEWIS: Mum says he's got wife problems or something.

DULCIE: It's because he lives in Singapore Street. There's something wrong with the water supply.

LEWIS: It tastes all right.

DULCIE: How do you explain the fact that every family in the street has had girls and you're the only boy? You have to be careful not to grow up to be a sissy, so Stan says.

LEWIS: Your Dad doesn't know what he's talking about. You laugh at me about UFOs, but this thing with water is just as strange. [Picking up brass casings] Come on, we don't have much time. [DULCIE helps him.]

SCENE TWO

Back veranda. Evening. There is the sound of crickets.

NARRATOR: Maybe Dulcie was right. Maybe there was something wrong with the water. I was the only boy in the street. Practically all my playmates were girls. Even at home it was all girls. My mother. My sister. My grandmother: she had come to stay when dad left us.

[Lights come up on LEWIS combing his grandmother's very long grey hair. He recites what she teaches him.]

GRANDMA: Bonnie Prince Charlie was born December 31 1720 and died January 31 1788

LEWIS: Bonnie Prince Charlie was born December 31 1720 and died January 31 1788.

GRANDMA: [half to herself] Died. [Getting carried away.] Died in ignominy because of the English. Reached as far as Derby. He could have easily taken London, if it wasn't for the French. The Frogs always let you down. Their support evaporated like rain on a hot tin roof.

[NORMA, Lewis' mother, enters.]

What were the dates of the rebellion?

LEWIS: 1745.

GRANDMA: And when did he take Edinburgh?

NORMA: Will you stop it, mum?

GRANDMA: Stop what?

NORMA: All this thing about English history.

GRANDMA: It's Scottish. I hate the English!

NORMA: [to LEWIS] Bonnie Prince Charlie was a drunkard.

GRANDMA: Out of disappointment!

NORMA: It's twelve thousand miles away. Dead history.

GRANDMA: Not to me. Not to millions of people who know England would be a better place if Bonnie Prince Charlie had ascended the throne. Dead history is Australian history. A few greedy miners get killed and it's called a civil war. A real civil war is like in England. Thousands upon thousands died. Now that's a Civil War.

NORMA: Just stop it, that's all, and put your budgie back in its cage. It's pooping everywhere.

GRANDMA: It's not like dog's poo; it's really small.

NORMA: It shits in our food.

GRANDMA: Charming. Charming language. Same as your father. Bad language and hating budgies go together. Like you and your no-hoper husband.

NORMA: Keep Eric out of this.

GRANDMA: Look at you. Lewis. Living in a housing commission house.

NORMA: You have no right to criticise me seeing you're living here.

GRANDMA: I have every right, I'm your mother. You've got brains and what happens? You run off with Irish scum and when I try to instil in Lewis the tiniest bit of refinement – [To LEWIS.] What side of a woman does a gentleman walk on?

LEWIS: Left hand side.

GRANDMA: Why?

LEWIS: To draw his sword more easily and to protect her dress if a passing carriage sprays mud.

NORMA: There are no carriages here. In case you haven't noticed we have cars.

GRANDMA: Don't talk down to me. And I pay to sleep on the couch.

NORMA: It's a divan.

GRANDMA: I give you my war widow's pension. So, here I am, surrounded by the scum of Australia. Thank goodness I have Sam.

NORMA: It's a bloody budgie.

GRANDMA: At least it doesn't talk to me like you do.

NORMA: One day I'm going to bite off its head. Now clean up its shit!

GRANDMA: Charming. Double charming.

BEV: [entering] Sam again?

NORMA: Why are you home so late?

BEV: Talking to my girlfriends. [To LEWIS] Brenda saw you and Dulcie cuddling on the ground at the rifle range.

LEWIS: We were wrestling.

NORMA: You're not getting Dulcie into trouble, are you?

LEWIS: She is not my girlfriend. She jumped on me. We were just wrestling.

NORMA: Why are you so immature?

GRANDMA: You don't wrestle girls. Do you walk on her left side?

LEWIS: She jumped on me.

GRANDMA: [pointing] First star. Wish!

NORMA: Mum, I'm talking to Lewis. Go inside and clean up Sam's shit.

GRANDMA: [exiting] Charming. Double charming.

NORMA: Why don't you bring your schoolmates home?

LEWIS: I brought Brian home and she hits him over the head with my cricket bat.

BEV: He called me a slut.

NORMA: [to BEV] Go inside and wash for tea.

[BEV goes.]

I wish your father was here. At your age, Lewis, you don't wrestle girls, it can only lead to disaster.

LEWIS: I don't want to wrestle her. She's always hanging around. All I want to do is spot a UFO. The skies are full of them in America. I want to spot the first Australian UFO.

NORMA: If you ever develop a sense of humour like your father, I'll kill you.

[She goes.]

LEWIS: [looking heavenwards] Please...one land here...just here in the paddocks.

SCENE THREE

The back garden of the Irvin's house. STAN, Dulcie's stepfather, is sitting in a colourful canvas chair, finishing off a beer, listening to the news on his transistor.

RADIO: The issue of whether Russia will remove its missiles from Cuba will be debated in the United Stations today. President Kennedy said this morning that there will no compromise with the Russians–

STAN: Absolutely not, blast them to smithereens

RADIO: –and he has given a deadline to the Russians to remove the missiles or if they don't the United States government will regard the Russian's non-compliance as an act of war–

STAN: Blast Cuba out of the water.

[He switches off the transistor, gulps down the last of his beer and calls out.]

Is there any more?

MRS IRVIN: [from inside] No.

STAN: [to himself] Christ. Have to go down to the pub. [LEWIS enters.]

LEWIS: Hello, Mr Irvin.

[Silence.]

STAN: What are you doing here?

LEWIS: Picking up Dulcie. We're going to the pictures.

STAN: Dulcie said you two saw Brian's father down at the rifle range.

LEWIS: He was shooting.

STAN: Well, that's what you'd do at a rifle range, isn't it? He owes me money. Has a bee in his bonnet about owing it to me. Probably wants to do me in. Is he a good shot? [LEWIS shakes his head.] You know, the world is a pig sty and if you ripped off the front of the houses you'd find swine. Oink. Oink. [He laughs at unsettling LEWIS.] You ready to join up?

LEWIS: Join up?

STAN: To fight the communists. Cuba. Russia. The start of World War Three. The Yanks will protect us. They're sending their new secret plane to Australia. It's like a flying wing. No fuselage. Modern. Deadly. Enough nuclear bombs to wipe out all the swine. It's an exciting time to be living in.

LEWIS: Yes. There was this Brazilian farmer. He had pigs. Swine. He was on television. He was taken aboard a flying saucer and forced to have sex with an alien.

STAN: A man or a woman alien.

LEWIS: A woman, of course.

STAN: The world is heading towards obliteration because of the Reds and all that's in your head is some Brazilian pig farmer knocking off some sheila from outer space. You know why I let you go out with Dulcie? Because although you're weird, you're safe, Lewis. A grade poofter safe. [MRS IRVIN enters.]

MRS IRVIN: Stan!

STAN: It's true. [To LEWIS] She doesn't go to the pictures to meet other boys, does she?

LEWIS: No.

STAN: There you are – same as in jail. Always trust a nancy boy. I'm going to the pub.

[He goes.]

MRS IRVIN: Dulcie won't be long. How's your mum?

LEWIS: Okay.

MRS IRVIN: I've got something special to show her in Church on Sunday. [She takes out a small plastic container and shows it to LEWIS.]

LEWIS: What is it?

MRS IRVIN: A piece of bone. Very special bone. From St Thomas. A holy Relic. It cost me and arm and a leg to get it. Blessed by the Pope.

LEWIS: It's a bit small.

MRS IRVIN: It's not as if I could have bought a rib or thigh bone, Lewis. There are a lot of Catholics in the world and St Thomas was a very small man. This'll go next to my bed. At the feet of my Madonna lamp. The bone will connect me to God, he'll answer my prayers. Give a child to Stan and me. Do you pray?

LEWIS: Around exam time I pray a bit.

[DULCIE comes out wearing lipstick.]

DULCIE: Ready.

MRS IRVIN: Get that off now.

DULCIE: Why?

MRS IRVIN: You know why. Make-up is a temptation to men. At your age you should be beyond temptation. [DULCIE wipes off the lipstick with her handkerchief.] That's better.

DULCIE: Can I have some money?

MRS IRVIN: Wait a moment. [She goes inside.]

LEWIS: Your mum's always on about having a child to Stan.

DULCIE: Christ knows why. He always beats her up. All he is is a dumb convict. What she sees in him is beyond me.

MRS IRVIN: [entering with purse, giving DULCIE money.] Ticket and icecream.

DULCIE: Ta.

MRS IRVIN: [withholding it] On condition that you and Stan stop fighting.

DULCIE: I don't fight him, he fights me.

MRS IRVIN: It's hard being a stepfather.

[Pause.]

DULCIE: All right, I'll try.

MRS IRVIN: [giving her money] And I want you to come to Church more often. Only heathens and Moslems don't go to Church.

DULCIE: I'll become a Moslem, then.

MRS IRVIN: I wish you wouldn't joke about those things.

DULCIE: [to LEWIS] Let's go.

[They go.]

MRS IRVIN: [looking at bone] Please...St Thomas... one child, that's all...just one sharing of our flesh...

NARRATOR: Even in Church she was more intense than all the others and I knew she was praying, praying so hard I thought she'd make herself ill, knowing she only had one prayer: to have another child. One that would make her husband grow close to her again.

SCENE FOUR

The paddocks. Afternoon.

NARRATOR: It's late afternoon. After the matinee. Over there is the graveyard. You have to cross through it to get to the pictures. Over there is the migrant hostel. Newly arrived from Europe, they lived in Nissen huts. There, through the paddocks is our school. And near it is the church. I'm standing in paddocks we called the crossroads where all these journeys: to the pictures, the hostel, the school, the church, the graveyard, the rifle range bisected.

[DULCIE and LEWIS are walking back from the pictures. She is rubbing off lipstick she obviously applied on the way to the cinema.]

We have just seen a double bill. One about a woman who married a man from outer space and one about the lost city of Atlantis.

DULCIE: A death ray couldn't kill that many people.

LEWIS: Yes, it could. Like a nuclear bomb.

DULCIE: There were no such things as death rays in those days. [Referring to lipstick] Is it all off?

LEWIS: A bit on the side.

    [She wipes it off.]

DULCIE: She treats me like a child. I'm practically a woman. [LEWIS picks up a stick.] What are you doing?

LEWIS: For snakes. I saw one around here in the paddocks. Brown. Black ones. Tiger snakes down near the creek.

DULCIE: Is that what you were doing last night, looking for snakes?

LEWIS: You were spying on me?

DULCIE: I was just out and about. My room was too hot. I felt like a Tom cat.

LEWIS: How could you see snakes in the night? I was looking for UFOs.

DULCIE: Do you do it every night?

LEWIS: When I've got asthma.

DULCIE: I want to come with you. So you knock on my window and come and get me.

LEWIS: But I don't want to.

DULCIE: Yes, you do. Let's get back to my place, I'll show you some stuff I shoplifted.

LEWIS: I'm waiting for Brian. We're going to play cricket.

DULCIE: He's such an idiot. Always got sex on his mind. That's what all men think of – except you. I'm going to leave school, become a prostitute. You call me – right? Knock on my window.

    [She spots BEATRICE, a Dutch girl, standing in the distance.]

That's that wog girl you have to sit next to, isn't it?

LEWIS: Yes.

DULCIE: [throwing stone at her] Bloody wogs! Get back to the migrant hostel. [To LEWIS] Eye-ties.

LEWIS: She's Dutch.

DULCIE: Same difference. [Yelling to BEATRICE] Get back to your dykes! [The girl moves away.] If you don't keep them away, pretty soon they take over everything. Jobs. Shops. [Smiling] You can become my hoon. [She heads off, shouts back, pretending to step on a snake] Snake! Snake! Help me, Lewis.

[He half goes to help. She laughs and exits. The migrant girl, BEATRICE, wanders back now that DULCIE has gone.]

NARRATOR: During that year our school received a lot of migrants. But we didn't mix with them. Because of overcrowding I had to sit next to one. A Dutch girl, Beatrice, who had just arrived. 'Typical', I thought, 'wogs always arrived at the wrong end of the year and then didn't know a word of English'. Beatrice always wore her jumper – even on the hottest days.

[BEATRICE waves coyly to LEWIS, then comes over.]

LEWIS: [to himself] Oh, no. [He looks around to make sure no one can see him with her.]

BEATRICE: Hello, Lewis.

LEWIS: I see enough of you in class, nick off.

[Not understanding, she doesn't take offence.]

BEATRICE: [in Dutch] What are you doing?

LEWIS: Why don't you learn English?

BEATRICE: [in Dutch] That girl doesn't like me.

LEWIS: Go and play with your mates. That's what you do in Australia.

BEATRICE: [recognising the word] Australia?

LEWIS: Yes, look at you. It's boiling hot and you've got a jumper on. Take it off. Don't you know anything?

BEATRICE: [in Dutch, pointing] I saw a snake over there.

LEWIS: Take it off. [He attempts to take off her jumper.]

BEATRICE: [in Dutch] What are you doing?

LEWIS: That's why you're sweating like a horse.

BEATRICE: [in Dutch] It's from Holland.

LEWIS: Use your hand. You wogs can be really stupid. Look! [Using Nazi accent] You are not a Nazi now. You are in

Australia. You are free to take off your jumper. I command you to take it off.

[He grabs it, then realises there is no arm.]

Where's your other arm?

[He lifts up her jumper where there is only a stump where her arm should be. She notices his shock and hurriedly and ashamedly puts her jumper back on. BRIAN enters.]

BRIAN: [calling out] You playing with wogs now, Lewis?

LEWIS: [quietly, pushing her away] Nick off.

BRIAN: Wogs aren't like us.

LEWIS: But you're a wog.

BRIAN: No, I'm not.

LEWIS: Your mother's Italian.

BRIAN: Dad's just as Australian as your dad. It's mum that forced him into marriage. She said that if dad didn't marry her she'd get her brothers to kill him – they're in the Mafia. Anyway, it's the dick that counts; if your father's Australian, then you are. Got it? [LEWIS nods.] It's not even as if we eat wog food or anything, I mean dad's insisted on that. [Referring to the stick] What's that for?

LEWIS: [throwing it away] Nothing.

BRIAN: Go to the pictures with Dulcie?

LEWIS: Yes.

BRIAN: Shagged her yet?

LEWIS: [offended] No.

BRIAN: Felt her norks yet?

LEWIS: There's nothing special about women.

BRIAN: Don't you ever want to touch them? God, I can't sleep at night. Just dreaming of touching them. Know why I take the bus home? 'Cos when we come to a stop I pretend to stumble, bam! I accidentally, on purpose, fall into one of the women. I touch their tits real quick, like this...

LEWIS: You touch the women's tits?

BRIAN: They're not women, they're housewives.

LEWIS: They must know you're doing it.

BRIAN: Some of them really like it. I told Dad. He said I was going to be a real tit man like him.

LEWIS: I saw your dad on the shooting range.

BRIAN: I think he wants to kill a warder who gave him a tough time in prison.

LEWIS: Dulcie's dad is after him.

BRIAN: He wants to kill him too. Threepence should be enough.

LEWIS: For what?

DULCIE: To feel up Dulcie. I'll pay her. You ask her for me.

LEWIS: I can't ask her. [Using BEATRICE to get onto another topic] You know that wog girl. She hasn't got an arm. That's why she keeps her jumper on. She's just got a stump. It's kind of got a knot of skin at the bottom, like it's been tied up. I felt it.

BRIAN: You felt her stump? [LEWIS nods.] You're sick, you know that. All I want to do is feel Dulcie's tits. It's a natural thing. I don't go around feeling stumps. Look, don't even talk to wogs. They lead you into unnatural things. Like their food. Or feeling their stumps. Just be normal, Lewis.

   [They exit.]

BEATRICE: [calling] Lewis! [But he doesn't hear. She picks up his stick and heads off, banging the ground to keep away snakes. Passing her, but going the other way, as if following LEWIS, is a JAPANESE WOMAN wearing a rich, red kimono. BEATRICE passes within inches of her but it's as if she doesn't see her.]

SCENE FIVE

The backyard of DULCIE's home. It is night and LEWIS enters carrying a pillow.

LEWIS: [calling softly] Dulcie...Dulcie...

DULCIE: Shhh...

   [He is puzzled – where did that shhh come from?]

LEWIS: Dulcie?

[Suddenly, as if flying, she appears, upside-down, like a glorious bat, swinging with the air.]

DULCIE: Catch me!

[She laughs at his surprise, as she hangs upside-down on a homemade trapeze swing.]

Will you catch me if I fall?

LEWIS: What are you doing up there?

DULCIE: Shhh...He's just gone to sleep. Drunk as a skunk. Did you bring the pillow? [He holds it up.] It hasn't got sponge in it, it's got real feathers?

LEWIS: That's what you asked for. I had to steal it from my sister. [She laughs.] We've got two choices. Wait here and watch the skies or go down to the power station.

DULCIE: Why the power station?

LEWIS: It's where they get their energy from.

DULCIE: They might not need earth energy.

LEWIS: It was on a radio interview with a scientist who said he had traced the grids of their flight path and they were all centred around power stations.

DULCIE: Sounds stupid to me.

LEWIS: Why do you want to come with me then?

[She swings back and forth hanging from her legs, her dress falling down, seemingly not aware that her panties are showing.]

DULCIE: I like to get out of the house. I like being with you. You know why God likes me, because he gave me the only tree in the whole district and it's here in my backyard because he knows I want to be an acrobat. You go onto the other trapeze.

LEWIS: I want to go to the power station.

DULCIE: We were going to be trapeze artists

LEWIS: You never got a net.

DULCIE: You landed wrongly. Come up, see the UFOs from here. [He clambers up on the other swing, she fingers a caterpillar pod.] A caterpillar pod. That's what we are: caterpillars waiting to turn into angels.

[He laughs.]

Shhhh....

[Silence.]

An angel is passing. He's stopping and he's listening to us and we explain the beauty and suffering of our world but we can't explain it properly. We only mumble, stumble, not make sense. The angel understands though and he presses his lips against my hand. [She grabs LEWIS' hand and presses her lips against it.] He says a word into my hand. What is that word, Lewis? [He shakes his head.] The angel is hurt, you aren't listening?

LEWIS: My bum's sore. [He hops down from the swing.]

DULCIE: [to the heavens] Allah, be praised! I've decided to become a Moslem so I don't have to go to Church with mum. She doesn't know how to deal with it. I said that if she forces me to go to mass, I'm going to bend down in the aisle and shout out 'Allah, be praised!' Embarrassing, eh?

[A beat.]

You're taking me to the fancy dress party.

LEWIS: Fancy dress party?

DULCIE: The break-up party. Dad said you're the only boy he trusts me with.

[A beat.]

If I fall, will you catch me?

LEWIS: No. [Pause.] I stole the pillow for you. I'm taking you to the break-up party, so you have to return a favour for me.

DULCIE: Whatever.

LEWIS: Show your chest to Brian.

DULCIE: My chest?

LEWIS: He wants to see it.

DULCIE: He wants to see my tits?

LEWIS: You said you'd repay the favour. [A beat.] Threepence, he'll pay you.

DULCIE: Threepence?

LEWIS: Sixpence then.

   [Pause.]

DULCIE: Why didn't you say no, I wouldn't do it?

LEWIS: He said I wouldn't be his friend any more.

   [She jumps down from the swing, almost as if she is going to hit him. He backs away. She grabs the pillow in a fury.]

DULCIE: All right, then. If I do that for you, you have to wear what I make for the break-up party.

LEWIS: Sure. [She thumps him one.] What's that for?

DULCIE: God males are thick. [She goes inside leaving a perplexed LEWIS behind.]

SCENE SIX

LEWIS' backyard, not long afterwards. GRANDMA is looking at the sky, lost in thought. The NARRATOR, as if he is younger LEWIS, watches her, asking questions.

GRANDMA: Too many...too many falling.

NARRATOR: What are you doing out this late, Grandma?

GRANDMA: There are less stars than I remember. When I was young there were more. [Pause.] A curious thing happened to me. I was washing, preparing for bed and I looked in the mirror. I couldn't recognise myself. So old. So wrinkled. I said, 'Who are you?' And this ancient crone asked me 'Who are you?' What are you doing up so late?

NARRATOR: UFO spotting.

GRANDMA: [as if it is the most normal thing] Oh, yes. Did you see any?

LEWIS: [entering] no.

GRANDMA: [turning to him] Is anything the matter?

LEWIS: Girls are hard to figure out.

GRANDMA: There is only one thing to know in life. Love for a woman is surrender. Love for men is victory. And who ever hears of the victor and the defeated living in harmony. [A beat.] It's so hot. So hot. No rain. Soon we'll be slipping in between the cracks in the soil. [A beat.] It's because of the sputniks. The Russians are deliberately interfering with the sky. The sputniks dent the atmosphere. Softening us up before going to war against the Russians. Over Cuba! It just grows sugar. We grow sugar.

[As they overhear a domestic dispute from next door, LEWIS, whose asthma has flared up, takes out his spray and uses it.]

MAN: Get off my back!

WOMAN: You come home drunk!

MAN: I come home pissed.

WOMAN: Spent all the money.

MAN: Well, I bloody well earned it.

WOMAN: You're a real bastard

MAN: Get off my back!

WOMAN: Bastard! Bastard!

MAN: [hitting the WOMAN] Shut up!

[The WOMAN weeps.]

LEWIS: [between gasping breaths] The Harrisons.

GRANDMA: See what I said. [She grabs his spray, he automatically opens his mouth and she starts spraying his throat.] The two can't live together. Some neighbourhood your mother ended up in Lewis.

[They pause and listen to NORMA singing *Some Enchanted Evening* from South Pacific.]

Your mother...her husband's left her, she's living on practically nothing, and it looks like we'll soon have a nuclear war – but she's singing. Amazing.

[Pause as she stops spraying.]

Feeling better?

[He nods.]

Let's go inside.

SCENE SEVEN

The crossroads. Day. MR PISANO is doing his mail round, only this time he is jogging without a shirt. BRIAN doesn't notice him because he is preoccupied in obliterating bull-ants by using a magnifying glass. BEATRICE is in the background watching him, thinking she is unnoticed, but PISANO notices her.

PISANO: [yelling out to BEATRICE] Tell your wog friends to address their envelopes in English or else I'm coming nowhere near that hostel. [Noticing BRIAN.] So, what are you doing, Master B. Johnson?

BRIAN: Killing bull-ants with my magnifying glass. When they burn they really shrivel up. Someone steal your shirt, Mr Pisano?

PISANO: I'm getting a suntan, what does it look like? Got your father's intelligence. I saw him down by the rifle range this morning.

BRIAN: He's practising to kill someone, maybe my mother's brothers, maybe the cop who put him in jail last time.

PISANO: Whoever he wants to shoot, they'll be safe. He couldn't hit the side of a barn. [He jogs off as LEWIS enters.]

LEWIS: Are postmen allowed to take off their uniforms?

BRIAN: Pisano's a law unto himself. He's got a bit looney because his wife is rooting other men. Talking of roots, what time is Dulcie showing up?

LEWIS: She said she'd be here. [Spotting BEATRICE]. Damn.
    [She waves to him.]

BRIAN: Aren't you going to feel her stump?

LEWIS: [throwing stone at her] Get back to the hostel!
    [The stone hits her and she cries out in pain.]

BRIAN: [unconcerned] Why don't you throw like that when we play cricket?

LEWIS: Go on, back to the hostel!
    [Hurt, she goes]

BRIAN: What's she doing outside the hostel? I didn't think they let them out on weekends. Don't they have guards?

LEWIS: [spotting DULCIE] Hi.

[She is in a foul mood and says nothing. Silence.]

DULCIE: [holding out hand to BRIAN.] The money.

[BRIAN fumbles and gives it to her.]

DULCIE: It's only sixpence.

BRIAN: [to LEWIS] That's what you said.

DULCIE: For two tits, twice the money.

BRIAN: A shilling?

DULCIE: A shilling.

BRIAN: [reluctantly giving it to her.] Highway robbery.

[Pause.]

DULCIE: Not enough.

BRIAN: Give it back.

DULCIE: Two shillings.

BRIAN: Hey!

DULCIE: Two bob.

LEWIS: [handing over a shilling] Here.

BRIAN: Hey, thanks, Lewis.

DULCIE: [to LEWIS] Hoon.

BRIAN: Come on, we've paid up.

[DULCIE opens her blouse. BRIAN is impressed. LEWIS tries not to look.]

Great. Great.

DULCIE: Get it over with.

BRIAN: Eh?

DULCIE: Touch them. It's included in the price.

[As he touches them DULCIE looks at LEWIS barely able to contain her anger with him.]

Ugh, your palms are sweaty.

[She shoves him out of the way. Pause.]

Lewis.

BRIAN: It was for me.

DULCIE: Lewis paid half.

BRIAN: It wasn't long enough.

DULCIE: Lewis.

[He shakes his head.]

BRIAN: Another feel for me, then.

DULCIE: You've had enough.

BRIAN: Suppose a fuck's out of the question?

DULCIE: You'd be even quicker.

[She buttons up her blouse.]

BRIAN: Ten bob. A pound. A pound's as high as I go.

DULCIE: I couldn't stand your clammy hands.

[Pause.]

BRIAN: [referring to magnifying glass] Could you stand this?

DULCIE: What do you mean?

BRIAN: If I burnt you with this?

DULCIE: You couldn't hurt me.

BRIAN: You'd give up in a second.

DULCIE: Try me.

BRIAN: Hold out your arm.

[She holds out her arm. He turns it over and, getting it in the right position, lets the sun's rays pour through the glass.]

LEWIS: What are you two idiots doing?

BRIAN: She'll give up.

DULCIE: No, I won't.

[To LEWIS] Never.

[To BRIAN] If I don't give in Lewis has to feel my tits.

BRIAN: [to LEWIS] You can't lose. Hurting?

DULCIE: No.

[To LEWIS] How does it feel to be a hoon?

LEWIS: Stop it, her skin is burning.

BRIAN: She's enjoying this, aren't you?

DULCIE: [trying to keep from showing her pain.] Yes.

BRIAN: [pleased] It's really burning. Like the bull-ants! [A beat.] Give in?

DULCIE: No. [To LEWIS, loudly] Hoon! Pimp!

LEWIS: Stop it!

BRIAN: When she gives in.

DULCIE: I won't give in.

BRIAN: There's smoke! It's burning like a roast! Give in?

DULCIE: [shouting defiantly] No!

[Shouting at LEWIS] Hoon!

[LEWIS pushes BRIAN away, he tumbles to the ground.]

BRIAN: Hey!

DULCIE: What did you do that for?

LEWIS: You're both crazy.

DULCIE: He could have burnt all the way to my bone and I wouldn't have given in.

BRIAN: [wanting to continue] Okay, let's see how tough you are.

LEWIS: [wanting to distract BRIAN] This is boring, let's go and play cricket.

BRIAN: [shrugging] All right.

[As if DULCIE is not there, the two boys head off.]

DULCIE: [shouting after them] Fairies! Have your money. [She goes to throw the money but has second thoughts.] You don't buy me. I sell me. [The pain of the burn strikes her. She grimaces and rubs the sore spot. To herself.] Butter. I need some butter...

[She goes in search of butter.]

SCENE EIGHT

The backyard of LEWIS' house. NORMA is gardening. BEV is watching.

NORMA: The soil is like rock. [Looking at the garden] Nothing grows. The yard looks like a disused quarry. I don't even know why I try. Your father said he'd level this. Get some good soil and make it paradise. Paradise! And I believed him. Did you take one of my pillows?

BEV: Yeh, someone took mine.

NORMA: What do you mean, took it?

BEV: It's disappeared. [Spotting LEWIS entering] He's home. [To LEWIS] Boy, are you going to get it.

[NORMA is obviously annoyed with her son. She takes off her plastic washing gloves she uses for gardening.]

NORMA: Come here. [He comes over to her. She slaps him.] What kind of pervert am I bringing up?

LEWIS: What did you do that for?

NORMA: You and Dulcie were seen near the crossroads. What were you doing?

LEWIS: Nothing.

NORMA: Don't lie, Mrs Harrison saw you three.

LEWIS: We were playing cricket

NORMA: Lewis!

[Silence.]

LEWIS: Dulcie showed herself to Brian. It was just a bit of fun.

NORMA: Why did I have such a son. Lewis, what happens if you get her pregnant?

LEWIS: I didn't touch her.

NORMA: I really hate your father. He should be here. He should have told you about sex. [A beat.] Why do you make me hit you? I don't like hitting you. You're supposed to be the man of the household and all you're interested in is flying saucers and sex. Did you touch her?

LEWIS: No. Brian did.

[Pause.]

NORMA: Mrs Irvin and I have had a talk. We think it's better that you and Dulcie don't spend so much time together. It's unhealthy. Spend more time with boys.

LEWIS: I try to but Beverley keeps on hitting them over the head with cricket bats. They won't come anywhere near this house.

BEV: I told you what he called me.

NORMA: Beverley!

[There is going to be a flare up but something stops her. It is like a vision: a beautiful JAPANESE WOMAN, wearing a

kimono comes from out of nowhere. The trio is astonished.]

NARRATOR: Then, into my world of paddocks and Scotch thistles, came a woman. She was as exotic and foreign as an alien from outer space.

[GRANDMA comes out with a chair. The JAPANESE WOMAN sits on it. BEVERLEY gives the woman a cup of tea. Everyone stares at her. She smiles at them, holding the cup but not drinking. Then UNCLE RICHARD, wearing a cravat and moustache, and looking very bohemian, arrives.]

NORMA: Where did you get her, Richard?

RICHARD: Japan.

NORMA: But she doesn't speak English.

RICHARD: The perfect woman.

NORMA: [laughing] If you weren't my brother...

NARRATOR: Uncle Richard was in the theatre. You could tell because he wore a cravat. He visited us occasionally showing off his girlfriends. His previous one was Malayan, the one before that was from Siam. He liked exotic women, he said, because Western women wanted to be like men.

[The JAPANESE WOMAN giggles as she's being stared at.]

RICHARD: She makes great sushi.

NORMA: What's that?

RICHARD: Raw fish.

EVERYONE: Ugghhhh....

RICHARD: [miming drinking tea to her] You can drink.

[The JAPANESE WOMAN is self-conscious but she drinks. As she does so she makes loud slurping noises indicating her enjoyment. Everyone is astonished.]

LEWIS: Did you hear that! Did you hear that!

NORMA: She drinks like an animal, Richard.

[Everyone laughs. The JAPANESE WOMAN wonders why they are laughing but pretends happiness at pleasing them.]

RICHARD: The Japanese think it's polite to slurp their tea. It shows how much they enjoy it.

BEV: Gross. [TO JAPANESE WOMAN] More tea. More tea.

[The WOMAN drinks some more, leaving her witnesses entranced. UNCLE RICHARD leads LEWIS away so they can talk.]

RICHARD: Because your dad isn't here, Lewis, my sister wanted me to give you some advice. [Pause.] Lewis, in a place, a god forsaken suburb like this, it's easy to be average. I have a great fear that you'll be average. Don't be. Be different. Head and shoulders above the crowd. [Pause.] By the way, do you masturbate?

LEWIS: [embarrassed] No.

RICHARD: Well, start practising. Sex is like athletics, you have to keep your hand in before you start screwing girls. Now, another thing. Be firm with women. Be the boss, they like it. Without firmness they're like a compass needle spinning around wildly, endlessly searching for north. We are the magnetic pole for women. And another thing: oriental women are the best. Western women will only let you down.

[Pause as RICHARD waits for LEWIS' appreciation.]

LEWIS: Thank you, Uncle Richard.

RICHARD: Pleasure.

[UNCLE RICHARD goes inside. LEWIS turns around to see the JAPANESE WOMAN vanishing into the darkness from whence she came.]

NARRATOR: Then she went. Vanished from my world as if she were just a dream. Up until then I had never seen anything so exotic, so beautiful. I couldn't sleep that night. I had too much excitement. Too much advice. I went to look for UFOs. I headed towards the power station down Tobruk Street to the creek.

SCENE NINE

It is night in the paddocks. LEWIS is making slurping noises to himself like the JAPANESE WOMAN, enjoying the memory of her. He hears a noise and is nervous.

LEWIS: Yes? Who is it? I know someone's here. I can hear you.
[There is maniacal laughter.]
Who is it?
[Suddenly DULCIE leaps out of the darkness.]
DULCIE: Geronimo!
[She jumps on him and pins him to the ground.]
You hoon!
LEWIS: Get off. We're not allowed to see each other.
DULCIE: I want another pillow.
LEWIS: Why don't you take some from your own home?
DULCIE: Because ours are full of sponge. If you don't get me another pillow I'll tell everyone that you shagged me. Understand?
[He nods]
Understand?
LEWIS: Yes.
[She gets off him. They stand.]
DULCIE: Did you think it was a snake? [She laughs, heading off.] Tomorrow. The pillow! [To the heavens.] Allah, be praised!
[She goes. LEWIS shakes his head at her behaviour. Then he looks at the sky, searching for UFOs.]
NARRATOR: I liked being near the power station, listening to the hum of the generator, looking at the sky, glad to be away from everyone: because people didn't make any sense at all.
[As if reading his mind]
What do you want to be, Lewis?
LEWIS: [answering his own thoughts] Cricketer in summer. Bowler. A leggie. In winter, play for Collingwood. Drive a

truck. Drive and drive and drive up the Hume Highway and not stop.

[Looking at sky.]

Nothing.

[He stands, ready to go.]

NARRATOR: I was about to go home when I heard a sound. A different sound. Like the humming of the power station, only louder, more low pitched. And the vibrations became so powerful that my insides shook.

[LEWIS looks in the direction of the noise which is slow, eerie and rumbling. He is open mouthed in astonishment as light, bright and powerful, fills the paddocks.]

LEWIS: [ecstatically] A flying saucer!

ACT TWO

SCENE ONE

LEWIS stands addressing the audience.

LEWIS: I was down at the power station. I worked out that's
where they came to fuel or maybe they are working out the
power grids of our planet. I was waiting in the long grass
when I heard a strange noise. I looked up in the sky and
there it was: a UFO. A giant flying saucer. Right overhead.
A real one. It made a sound like this. [Imitating sound] Then
it was gone. I rushed home. I woke my mother: 'I saw a
flying saucer. A real one.'

[Gradually we are aware that it is NORMA and GRANDMA
listening to LEWIS.]

She said, 'Come on, Lewis I'm trying to sleep'.

NORMA: I didn't.

LEWIS: You did.

NORMA: And that's what you told your Show and Tell class
today.

[He nods.]

Did the class laugh?

LEWIS: Yes.

GRANDMA: Your teacher?

LEWIS: [shaking his head] He said I had a vivid imagination.

GRANDMA: I despair.

LEWIS: So do I. It was as real as you are.

GRANDMA: [To NORMA] Do you know what he saw?

NORMA: Perhaps his teacher is right, perhaps he does have a
vivid imagination, there's nothing wrong with that.

GRANDMA: Nothing wrong with imagining a flying saucer? [A
beat.] I despair of both of you. Ignorance. [To NORMA] I told

you what would happen when you married Eric. Your intelligence would shrivel.

NORMA: Stop picking on me.

GRANDMA: I buy newspapers and does anyone in this household read them? You should be ashamed of yourself. [To LEWIS] You too.

LEWIS: I saw it as real as day. It was real. Real.

GRANDMA: It was an American plane. A flying wing.

LEWIS: No, it wasn't.

GRANDMA: It was in the paper this morning, Obviously even your teacher doesn't read the newspapers. Doesn't need to in this area.

LEWIS: It was a flying saucer.

GRANDMA: It's a new American plane. One that will beat the Russians.

   [She shows him the newspaper.]

BEV: [entering] My other pillow's gone.

NORMA: That's strange. Lewis, do you know anything about these missing pillows?

LEWIS: I'm having enough trouble with UFOs.

NORMA: [to BEV] I'll help you look for it.

   [They go off to look for it.]

LEWIS: [reading the newspaper] It didn't look like this. It wasn't a flying wing.

GRANDMA: It was. You have an overactive imagination. If you had stuck to learning the history I've been teaching you, you wouldn't be laughed at. What is James VI of Scotland sometimes called?

LEWIS: [immersed in reading newspaper, to himself] It didn't look like this.

NARRATOR: [answering for him] James the First of Great Britain.

GRANDMA: [snorting with derision] Great Britain!

NARRATOR: He hated witches and loved golf.

GRANDMA: Any man who hates witches and loves golf can't be all bad.

NARRATOR: I looked and looked at that picture of the flying wing. Maybe I had made a mistake. It still didn't stop me from believing in UFOs. Nothing could. The very idea that Americans could build a plane that looked like a flying saucer meant that more advanced civilisations were certain to have built one. [LEWIS goes off with the newspaper. GRANDMA is wrapped up in her own thoughts.]

GRANDMA: [to herself] Of course, a pommy King would have loved witches and hated golf.

[To LEWIS, even though he isn't there] Your grandfather loved golf...

SCENE TWO

BRIAN's backyard. He is stripped to the waist, using a chest expander.

BRIAN: Twelve. Thirteen. Fourteen. [Seeing LEWIS] Ninety-six, Ninety-seven. Ninety-eight. Ninety-nine. Hundred.

[He stops, panting as much as he thinks he should.]

LEWIS: That's pretty good.

BRIAN: Generally do two hundred. [A beat.] Boy, what a dickhead. Flying saucers! The whole class thinks you're a prize dickhead. Everyone's laughing at you. I don't even know why I'm seen with you. My mate, the looney. [A beat.] Find another interest. Bodybuilding. Here, try this.

[He gives it to LEWIS who tries it a couple of times but is ineffectual.]

Hopeless. Try this technique. My father taught it to me. Look at a light and concentrate.

LEWIS: There's no light.

BRIAN: The sun then. You stare at it and concentrate and you can do stuff you never dreamed of. So look at the sun.

LEWIS: I'll go blind.

BRIAN: Close your eyes then.

LEWIS: I can't see then.

BRIAN: Don't bloody bother.

[Brian snatches the chest expander from him. LEWIS takes a tennis ball out of his pocket and bowls it at BRIAN, but he is flummoxed because it spins the wrong way.]

LEWIS: A wrong 'un. I've taught myself to bowl a wrong 'un. It fooled you.

BRIAN: That's bloody typical, isn't it? Bowl fast, spin is for sissies.

LEWIS: You thought it was going to spin the other way.

BRIAN: Spin is for women, Lewis. It's devious. Full of betrayal. [Spotting his father] 'Bye, dad! [Loudly] 'Bye, dad.

LEWIS: Maybe he didn't hear you.

BRIAN: Probably. He's a bit depressed lately. Can't get a job.

LEWIS: I thought you said he'd never work.

BRIAN: Changed his mind. Came out of the clink a different person. If he goes in again, this time it'll be for years. A cop comes around a lot trying to get him back into the stolen car racket. Nothing more bent than a crooked cop. Dad wants nothing to do with him. He thinks it's a trap that the cop and Mr Irvin have set up for him to get him back into jail. He likes to go down to the rifle range a lot. He gained a funny sense of humour since he was last in the clink. Pointed his gun at me and said 'Start running, son'. I was about to piss off, he looked real mean, when he suddenly smiles and gives me a slug gun. That's what we should do. Go shooting. Plenty of cats around here, especially in Gallipoli street. Bang, right between the eyes. You got any money?

[LEWIS shakes his head]

There's this fella I know who'll sell me a few blue magazines. Hair and everything. Norks this big at a minimum. How can you control yourself, Lewis? [Watching LEWIS pick up the ball] You practise your bowling, I'm pulverising the python. Lately I've been thinking a lot about Dulcie while I'm doing it. Put a good word in for me with her, will you?

LEWIS: I haven't seen her for a week.

> [LEWIS bowls the spin ball at BRIAN who misses the wrong 'un again.]

BRIAN: Don't do that, it gives me the creeps. [A beat.] What about your sister, Bev? She'll do.

> [LEWIS is irritated.]

It's not as if I'm a rapist or anything. If you do that for me, I'll get you the Dutch girl: she can give you a hand job.

> [BRIAN laughs but it isn't funny to LEWIS.]

Hey, I'd thought you'd like that one. Let's get the slug gun and go and kill some cats. [They go.]

SCENE THREE

DULCIE's bedroom. She is looking at her reflection in a hand mirror, talking to herself.

DULCIE: Ugly. [Pulling faces] Beautiful. [Smiling] Fuck you. Fuck you, fuck you. [Poking out tongue] The ugliest girl in the whole world. I'm gonna smash up your face until it's pulp, spit pulp...

> [There is a knock at the window.]

Who is it?

LEWIS: Me.

DULCIE: Oh, it's you.

LEWIS: Can I come in?

DULCIE: Yes.

> [He comes in through the window.]

Be quiet. How long were you at the window?

LEWIS: Not long. Just enough to see you pulling faces at yourself.

DULCIE: You were spying on me.

LEWIS: I wasn't.

DULCIE: So why are you here?

LEWIS: I was with Brian. The Harrison's cat is no more. He blew it apart. He's off for the Hardy's.

DULCIE: So why aren't you with him?

LEWIS: I saw your mum going off for midnight mass. You said to knock on your window if you wanted to see UFOs.

DULCIE: I don't want to.

LEWIS: How was I to know? You haven't been to school for a week.

DULCIE: It's for deadshits.

LEWIS: The truant inspector'll get you.

DULCIE: Who cares? She's always threatening to send me to a Home. I hope she does so I can be out of here. She threatened me with it tonight, so I got down on the floor [demonstrating] and prayed to Allah. Allah be praised!

[They both laugh. A radio is turned on and although faint we can hear a news report on the Cuban crisis. The United Nations has been unable to resolve the crisis and many people are fearing a nuclear war.]

STAN: [off] Blast them to bits. Make Cuban bacon!

DULCIE: He's really drunk tonight.

[LEWIS notices a large hessian bag and some feathers poking out of it. He looks inside.]

LEWIS: These all from Bev's pillows?

DULCIE: Sure.

LEWIS: I thought you wanted the pillows to sleep on.

DULCIE: I want them for something special.

LEWIS: What?

DULCIE: You'll see. [A beat.] There's no such thing as UFOs.

[LEWIS shrugs and notices a doll.]

LEWIS: What have you done to it?

DULCIE: It's old. I was a child then. I don't like the way it looks so I put the arms where the legs should be and the legs where the arms should be. I'd like to put an arm where the head should be. Do you think I look ugly?

LEWIS: No.

DULCIE: My father was handsome. Very brown, shiny like copper. Tall. He was Basque, mum says. He went back to fight for the freedom of Basque. He died in a hail of bullets from the Spanish police. Have you shagged the Dutch girl yet?

LEWIS: I don't like her.

DULCIE: You don't have to like someone to shag them. [STAN starts singing loudly: *Goodnight, Irene.*] Really drunk. If there are flying saucers, why are they coming to earth?

LEWIS: To look us over. To observe us. In the same way we go to the zoo and look at anteaters.

DULCIE: What do these spacemen look like?

LEWIS: Same as us. But you can tell their real form during a storm. Lightning reveals their true form.

DULCIE: They take over human bodies?

LEWIS: According to the man who went to Venus.

DULCIE: How would they do that?

LEWIS: They're superior to us. They take over our minds. Our bodies.

DULCIE: Besides a storm, how else would you know they were aliens?

LEWIS: They'd try to be human. Sometimes, though, their true behaviour would be obvious.

DULCIE: They'd do strange things? Unhuman things?

LEWIS: Yes.

[Suddenly she grabs a carving knife and holds it against LEWIS' throat. He is frightened by her.]

LEWIS: What are you doing?

DULCIE: I am an alien. You found me out. We are like the Indians of America. [She grabs his hair and puts the knife to his scalp.] We scalp white men.

[The radio goes off.]

He's coming. You'd better go.

[He steps away.]

LEWIS: [referring to the knife] What are you doing with that thing?

DULCIE: [smiling broadly] An alien needs something in an emergency when he's found out. [A beat.] Hurry. You'd better go. He's coming down the hallway.

[LEWIS goes.]

SCENE FOUR

The backyard. LEWIS practising his bowling.

NARRATOR: In the long, hot Australian summer days there are signs of movement. And there I am, practising my bowling. The earth is cracked, the grass dead and the stumps is one of the washing line posts in the backyard. There are two posts, a couple of meters high, with clothes lines tied to both crossbars, so that the lines look like crucifixes. The ball, its leaving the hand, its drift and spin through the hot air, its fall and turn once it hits the ground is mesmerising. I bowl through the long afternoons thinking I am a famous cricketer. I'm thinking of a cat dying, Dulcie and her knife against my throat, she showing her breasts to Brian, Mrs Irvin and her piece of St Thomas's bone...but never my sister. A brother rarely thinks of his sister.

[BEV enters, watching LEWIS bowling.]

BEV: You're mad doing it this heat.

[He pays no attention to her.]

You took my pillows, didn't you?

[He pays no attention to her. MR PISANO comes running into the backyard, but running backwards]

PISANO: [giving letter to BEV as he runs on the spot] Don't even have your mother open it, it's only a bill.

BEV: Why are you running your round backwards, Mr Pisano?

PISANO: Why do I have to run forwards? There was this man who ran across America backwards. I'm in training, maybe I'll run across Australia backwards. I'm doing me round counter clockwise in the afternoon, the normal way in the morning. That way I kind of meet up with myself. Now I'm running late because I've had to come into your backyard. That indicates the urgent nature of my business. How many times do I have to tell you: the number has to be bigger!

[He goes.]

BEV: It's because his wife left him. That's why he's acting funny. She left him the other night. While she was putting her luggage into the taxi he was outside on the footpath begging her to stay. On his knees! Why are men so embarrassing.

[A distant song is heard sung by a man.]

ERIC:
    Many a tear has to fall
    But it's all in the game
    All in the wonderful game of love.

[A man appears. It is ERIC, LEWIS' father.]

LEWIS: Dad!

ERIC: Hi, kids!
    You had words with him
    And your future's looking dim
    But these things your heart
    Will fly above.

[He kisses them both and guides them into the house. They are happy. He keeps on singing.]

    Once in a while he won't call
    But it's all in the game.

NARRATOR: My mother always said that when he first dated her he would come singing *It's all in the Game* and leave at night singing *Carrickfergus*.

ERIC:
    Soon he'll be there
    With a small bouquet
    And he'll kiss your lips
    And caress your fingertips
    And your heart will fly away.

NARRATOR: He was back after three years. He hadn't changed that much. We children were glad to have him home, unlike my grandmother and, of course, my mother.

[Pause.]

I heard them in her bedroom that night. The door was open.

SCENE FIVE

The bedroom. Night.

NORMA: I didn't hear a word from you. You sent no money.

ERIC: Yes, I did.

NORMA: Once. What were you doing?

ERIC: Digging tunnels.

NORMA: Tunnels?

ERIC: The Snowy Mountains scheme.

NORMA: You know nothing about tunnels.

ERIC: I do now.

NORMA: What did you do with the money you earned?

ERIC: Caught the gambling bug.

NORMA: Was there another woman?

ERIC: There's always been only you.

NORMA: Come off it.

ERIC: Only you.

NORMA: Why did you leave then?

ERIC: Felt suffocated, I guess.

NORMA: Suffocated? You say, one day, that you're going out to get a screw for the shower and don't come back. I was worried frantic. The police came and everything. They were quite certain. 'He's run off,' they said, 'probably didn't like being a husband'. Nice coming from the police, isn't it?

ERIC: They were wrong.

NORMA: You ran away because of the children and me.

ERIC: I've come back.

NORMA: Hip hooray, let's strike up the band!
    [Pause.]
    You must hate me to do what you did.

ERIC: There's so many of you. You, the kids, now your mother's here.

NORMA: Because she pays board. [A beat.] You left because you hate me, you hate your children.

ERIC: I don't hate anyone. I just got itchy feet.

NORMA: Have you no sense of responsibility?

    [A beat.]

ERIC: Guess not.

    [Pause.]

NORMA: What are you going to do?

ERIC: Don't know. Might level the backyard –

NORMA: Level the backyard?

ERIC: You've always been after me to do it.

NORMA: You can't stay here, I don't want you any more.

    [A beat.]

ERIC: The kids liked me being back.

NORMA: Of course, they've forgotten what you're really like.
   They don't know how shiftless and lazy you are!

ERIC: I'm not that. I've changed my ways.

NORMA: Shhhh...

    [She's looking at the doorway. He turns to see what she's
    staring at. It is LEWIS looking at them.]

  What are you doing up at this hour, love?

LEWIS: Couldn't sleep.

NORMA: How long have you been standing there?

LEWIS: Not long.

ERIC: Why can't you sleep?

LEWIS: Asthma.

NORMA: How's your spray?

    [BEV enters.]

ERIC: Can't you sleep either, darl?

    [She shakes her head.]

LEWIS: You staying, dad?

ERIC: Depends on your mother. Hey...Toulouse Lautrec!

    [He gets down on his knees and starts waltzing around on
    his knees, an action which amuses his children. NORMA is
    determined not to be amused, not to show any weakness.
    He starts singing in a French accent, not unlike the
    cartoon character Pepe la Phew.]

I hate Paris in the summer/ I hate Paris in the fall/ Oh, why oh why do I hate Paris/ because pissoirs are for the tall.

[He walks past NORMA on his knees, eyeing her crotch.]

You see the most interesting sights when you're this height.

[He notices she is becoming irritated. He tries another approach. He gets up off his knees and becomes serious.]

I mean, your mum's been a wiz looking after you while I've been working. [She gives a small snort of derision.] An absolute Wiz. The Wiz of Oz. [Pulling out match and lighting it.] Get this.

[He puts the lighted match in his mouth and pulls it out again still burning, having not burnt his mouth. LEWIS and BEV applaud.]

BEV: Magic.

ERIC: Skill. A dago on the Scheme tried to do it after seeing me and burnt his mouth so badly it was like a burnt pork chop.

[Silence.]

Well, best I go.

[He makes no move to go.]

SCENE SIX

The crossroads. Day. The Dutch girl has a stick and is poking it in a crack in the soil when BRIAN comes along.

BRIAN: What are you doing, wog? [She smiles.] Why you poking the hole with a stick? A bloody snake, angry as hell, will come out and bite you. [He shakes his head at her stupidity.] It's like they only send out the stupid ones. [Changes tack.] That's right. Harder. Poke it around. In and out. Harder!

BEATRICE: [to BRIAN as she pokes] Bugger. Shit. Piss. Fuck.

[LEWIS enters surprised to see BEATRICE with BRIAN.]

BRIAN: Hey, you talking to me?

BEATRICE: [smiling.] Yes.

BRIAN: I'm going to bloody brain you.

[He advances on BEATRICE, she shrinks away. He notices LEWIS.]

Did you hear what she said to me?

BEATRICE: [Happy to see LEWIS.] Hello, Lewis. [A beat.] Bugger. Shit. Piss. Fuck.

BRIAN: She said the same to me.

LEWIS: It's all right, I taught her.

BRIAN: Taught her?

LEWIS: She's always here at the crossroads following me about so I taught her those words. She thinks its proper English. Sort of like teaching a parrot.

BRIAN: You're all right, Lewis. You're all right. [To BEATRICE] Bugger. Shit. Piss.

BEATRICE: Yes.

BRIAN: Amazing. [To LEWIS.] Want to go down to the rifle range?

LEWIS: Will your dad be down there?

BRIAN: Can't afford the bullets. He's in bed. Been there for a few days.

LEWIS: Is he sick?

BRIAN: No. He says he's thinking. He's got some plan. But, boy, he's getting moody. He comes into the kitchen last night and puts the rifle in his mouth and says he's going to pull the trigger. Mum got hysterical, you know how eye-ties get, but then he took it out and said he wouldn't because mum was too short to clean his brains from the ceiling. He said it was a joke but mum didn't think it was funny. She says dad was hit over the head once too often by a warder.

LEWIS: [teasing] Maybe he's been taken over by aliens?

BRIAN: [not understanding he's being teased] Don't go weird on me, too, Lewis.

BEATRICE: Bugger. Shit. Piss. Fuck.

BRIAN: How do you shut her up?

LEWIS: [miming] Poke stick in hole.

BRIAN: If there's a snake down there it's going to be as angry as hell.

[BEATRICE pokes stick in the hole aggressively.]

You know, when they built this estate we were one of the first families to shift in. Your street came last. Guess what dad did just after we shifted in? See, it was all paddocks, even where your house is now. So dad set fire to all the paddocks. Every year he's done that. Sort of like a Christmas present for us.

LEWIS: He didn't light the last two.

BRIAN: How could he? He was in the clink. Some copycat did it. So I said to him. Get in first before the copycat. Burn the paddocks. If he sets fire to them I reckon it will relieve a lot of his moodiness. Let's get some brass. Hey, I hear your dad's come back.

LEWIS: He said he's staying for good. [Noticing BEATRICE is about to follow.] Stay here. You can't come. [They start to go.]

BEATRICE: [calling out.] Lewis!

[They turn around. She starts to take off her jumper.]

LEWIS: Keep it on, I don't want to see your stump. [To BRIAN as they walk off.] She's strange.

BRIAN: It's like females are not human, isn't it?

BEATRICE: [irritated at being ignored, pokes the hole angrily.] Shit. Fuck. Piss. Bugger. Bugger. Bugger. Fuck...

SCENE SEVEN

Night. ERIC is sitting under the house with a torch humming to himself *It's all in the Game*. LEWIS crawls under also carrying a torch.

LEWIS: Dad...dad...

ERIC: Over here. And keep your voice down.

LEWIS: Why are we under the house?

ERIC: Shhhh...Listen. Your mother's footsteps. Pretty heavy for a small woman. You can hear your grannie snoring. Women hate being underground. It scares them. That's why men love being underground. Be away from women. You should have seen the tunnels we dug in the Snowy Mountains. Right through granite like a knife through butter. Day after day we blew up the rock with dynamite, inching our way down for the good of Australia. It got hotter as we got deeper. We dug past fossils from dinosaur days. It was hard to breathe it was so deep. A lot of strange things happen in tunnels.

LEWIS: What sort of thing?

ERIC: Can't go into details right now. [A beat.] When you're older. We could dig a tunnel – just the two of us – under the house and come out under the Irvin's floorboards. Boy, would they be surprised. That girl you like, Dulcie or whatever, you could come up through her bedroom floor. Her eyes would be as big as saucers. [He starts to crawl under the house with the candle, exploring the space.] A lot of space...We could dig a tunnel through the floorboards into Castro's bedroom, Probably while he's knocking off some Russian sheila.

LEWIS: What exactly are we doing, dad?

ERIC: We're being quiet, that's what we're doing. [Footsteps above.] I can always tell your mother's footsteps. Doesn't realise what we've got in store for her. Women always expect the worst from a man.

[A pause as they listen to NORMA singing a snatch of a song.]

NORMA: Step we gaily on we go
                      heel and heel
                      and toe for toe
                      arm and arm
                      and row and row
                      all for Marie's wedding.

ERIC: [a pause as they listen to the footsteps] Bit of a bounce in her footsteps Probably thinking of me. Hey, it's lucky we're white, isn't it? How do blacks see one another in the dark? Like those West Indian cricketers eh? I saw them in the tied Test.

LEWIS: I thought you were in the Snowy Mountains?

ERIC: I was up in Brisbane for a while. Had to see a man about a tunnel. The West Indians were like gods. [Stopping, looking around] A lot of work ahead of us. Our little Snowy Scheme right under your mother's feet. Twinkle, twinkle little star, sixteen days and there you are. Always remember that rhyme, Lewis. It's how long it took Bert Hinkler to fly to Australia from London. My father taught it to me. [Hearing something] That bloody budgie. Something should be done about it. You know what happened in the second world war [LEWIS shakes his head.] Those fellers wanted to escape from the Nazis, so they built a wooden horse, an exercise horse, to dig a tunnel. The problem was: how to get rid of the soil so that the krauts didn't know what was happening. So they put the soil up their trousers and secretly sprinkled it on the parade ground. That's us, Lewis. We're the POWS and your mum's the kraut. In sixteen days we're going to give her the bestest birthday present.

SCENE EIGHT

Backyard of DULCIE's house. She is swinging upside-down on her trapeze, singing to herself. LEWIS enters and watches her for a time. She pretends she doesn't see him watching her.

DULCIE: Will you catch me if I fall?

LEWIS: No.

[She swings back and forth deliberately provocative in showing her panties.]

DULCIE: Maybe they're worms

LEWIS: Worms?

DULCIE: The aliens. They turn into small worms, crawl into your mouth, your arse, through your ears and into your brain and take over your mind.

MRS IRVIN: [entering] Dulcie! Get down! [Spotting LEWIS] What are you doing here?

DULCIE: I asked him.

MRS IRVIN: Why can't you behave like a lady!

DULCIE: Because I'm not one.

MRS IRVIN: Get down and put some shorts on if you're going to do that.

DULCIE: There's nothing wrong with what I'm doing. Rats do it.

MRS IRVIN: Get down.

DULCIE: No.

MRS IRVIN: Don't ever say no to me.

DULCIE: No, no, no. No!

MRS IRVIN: I want you to go, Lewis.

DULCIE: No, stay!

MRS IRVIN: You little vixen. Take after your father. Dirty mind.

DULCIE: I have a dirty mind. I have a dirty mind. I have a dirty mind.

MRS IRVIN: Go inside.

DULCIE: He probably hated your bullshit too.

MRS IRVIN: Wash out your mouth.

DULCIE: Piss off.

MRS IRVIN: May God strike you down.

DULCIE: Bullshit on your old bones.

MRS IRVIN: [jumping up and hitting her legs] Tramp! Foul mouthed tramp. You're showing your true colours now. Stan will strap some sense into you.

DULCIE: He'll have to catch me first.

MRS IRVIN: He'll strap you so hard.

DULCIE: If he straps me again...If he comes into my room... [Silence.]

MRS IRVIN: He can control you, which is more than a lot of people can. [Quietly] You go home, Lewis.

DULCIE: He's the only friend I've got.

MRS IRVIN: The way you two behave you should have no friends.

LEWIS: [embarrassed by all of this] I might go now.

DULCIE: Stay.

MRS IRVIN: He wants to go. Even he doesn't like you.

DULCIE: He likes me. You like me, don't you?

LEWIS: Yes.

DULCIE: [triumphantly] See...

MRS IRVIN: [to LEWIS] I'm going to talk to your mother.

[DULCIE is afraid of not being able to be with LEWIS again.]

DULCIE: [crying out.] I'll be good.

[Pause.]

MRS IRVIN: Will you?

DULCIE: [getting down from the swing] Yes.

[MRS IRVIN hits DULCIE across the face.]

MRS IRVIN: Your foul black mouth.

[DULCIE pretends the slap hasn't hurt.]

You deserve the strap you're going to get. [Referring to DULCIE.] She's almost beyond praying for.

[To LEWIS.] But I'll pray for you.

LEWIS: Thanks, Mrs Irvin

[MRS IRVIN starts to go inside.]

DULCIE: [quietly to LEWIS.] Saturday night. [He nods in agreement.]

MRS IRVIN: Dulcie!

[DULCIE falls to the ground and starts praying.]

DULCIE: Allah be praised! Allah, be praised!

MRS IRVIN: Get inside.

DULCIE: I can't, I'm praying. Every Moslem has to pray five times a day.

MRS IRVIN: East is that way. Now get inside before I call Stan.

[She reluctantly follows her mother inside.]

SCENE NINE

The front yard of a neighbour's house. Night. ERIC has a wheelbarrow. He enters, looking for the perfect spot to dig, then, realising that LEWIS is straggling reluctantly, signals for him to hurry up. Carting a spade, LEWIS enters.

ERIC: [gazing at stars]

Twinkle, twinkle little star

Sixteen days and there you are.

LEWIS: People will see us.

ERIC: They're watching TV or are asleep.

LEWIS: But they'll notice what we've done.

ERIC: It's not as if we're going to excavate the whole bloody front yard. We're nicking a bit from here, from the Johnson's, the Boyles.

LEWIS: But we'll leave a hole.

ERIC: Not a big one. They'll come out in the morning and think it was some animal.

LEWIS: What happens if we're caught?

ERIC: We'll say we're digging trenches as a last ditch stand against the Commies. Hey, how do you greet an American?

LEWIS: Don't know.

ERIC: [shaking LEWIS' hand] How ya doin', Yankee. How do you greet a Commie?

[LEWIS holds out his hand to be shaken.]

Like this!

[ERIC grabs his son by the arm and swings him over his shoulder, causing LEWIS to land on his back with a thud. LEWIS is winded. ERIC puts his foot on LEWIS' chest.]

Give up, Commie?

LEWIS: [winded] Yes.

ERIC: Like Commies, weak as piss. And what's the first lesson?

LEWIS: Don't know, dad.

ERIC: Never shake hands with a Communist unless you mean to do him harm. [Holding out hand] Come on, get up, we haven't much time.

> [LEWIS reaches for his hand suspiciously and his father lifts him up in one strong, violent pull.]

Sixteen days it is then. Fifteen now. Fifteen nights. We nick the Merri Creek soil from all the front yards that have it, then store it under our house. Night of your mum's birthday we level the backyard until it's as smooth as a baby's bum and flat as a billiard table. Don't you want to do that for your mum? [LEWIS nods.] Besides, we can build a cricket pitch on it. We'll be killing two birds with one stone. [A beat.] Dig, you dig?

NARRATOR: [as LEWIS digs] So, over the following night we stole soil from our neighbours' front yards. My father telling me stories of the Snowy Mountains, tunnelling from Victoria into New South Wales and of a dago trying to kill him with a dinosaur bone.

ERIC: Hang on. Let's rest a moment. You don't want to work like a wog, do you? They even worked through smokos. Had to take to them with a jack hammer. They could tell I wasn't scared of them when one of them tried to brain me with a dinosaur bone. [Looking around at the lawn] Pisano is a bit of a nutter, isn't he? I saw him mowing his lawn this morning but he's sort of just done bits of it. Holy Toledo! You know what he's done. He's mown a giant 45 into his lawn.

LEWIS: It's the number of his house. It's to teach the rest of the neighbourhood a lesson, he said.

ERIC: He's definitely not the full quid. This is good though, eh?

LEWIS: What?

ERIC: Us two. Father and son. Unnatural to have women around all the time. That thing between your legs, Lewis. Women go 'Oh, no, no!' but they always want it. Get them up the duff and it's our fault. You never hear the end of it.

> [LEWIS looks around, hearing something.]

What is it?

LEWIS: The telephone wires. It's like singing, isn't it?

[ERIC listens, he cannot understand his son's pleasure.]

ERIC: You're hearing things. You're at a difficult age. Your mum said Uncle Richard had a word to you.

LEWIS: He said I should marry a girl from Asia.

ERIC: Christ, we fought the slant eyes during the war and now he wants you to marry them. Forget it: he's a bit of a poof anyway. The important things are practical things. Shovel. Barrow. Soil. Rubbers. Don't forget them. If you fiddle about with that Dulcie, wear a rubber. Otherwise it's tragedy time. Your thing can be your downfall. It's a man's tragedy. Our Greek tragedy. [Motioning him back to work] Back on the chain gang.

LEWIS: It's rock hard.

ERIC: It needs more water. Put the hose on it.

LEWIS: His hose?

ERIC: Well, we're not going to go home and get ours, are we?

[LEWIS picks up hose and goes to turn it on, then suddenly he spots something.]

LEWIS: Dad! [ERIC looks around.] Someone at the window!

ERIC: Damn!

LEWIS: What'll we do?

ERIC: Piss off, that's what we'll do.

LEWIS: He's seen us!

ERIC: Don't be a sis: he hasn't! The wheelbarrow! The wheelbarrow!

LEWIS: [panicking] He's seen us.

ERIC: Come on.

[They rush off with their equipment as PISANO comes out. He peers into the darkness then sees the figures.]

PISANO: Hey you! What were you doing in my yard.

[He goes to run after them but trips over the hose.]

Damn.

SCENE TEN

The backyard. Night. GRANDMA is wandering in the back yard brooding, confused.

GRANDMA: [to herself] James was a Scottish King who believed in witches. He killed many at the stake. Before he went to play golf.

> [LEWIS, dirt covering his overalls enters, tired and exhausted, wheeling his wheelbarrow. Grandson and grandmother are surprised to see each other.]

I think I'm going mad. [Pause.] There's so many things swirling around in my head. I'm forgetting everything. For a moment I had no idea who King James was. Look at that star. Mary Queen of Scots saw that star when she gazed out of the Tower. Eighteen years that bitch kept her there. Excuse my French. [A beat.] I think about these things and they preoccupy me and then I start hearing things. I lie on the couch and hear these noises under the house. I come out here to escape them. What are you doing up so late?

ERIC: [entering with spade] He's helping me.

GRANDMA: Do what?

ERIC: Practise.

GRANDMA: Some sort of racing?

ERIC: Tunnelling.

GRANDMA: He's not going to be a labourer.

ERIC: There's nothing wrong with that.

LEWIS: I'm tired. I'm going inside.

ERIC: Tomorrow night?

LEWIS: Can't, it's the break-up party.

ERIC: With Dulcie?

LEWIS: Yes.

ERIC: Remember Greek tragedy.

LEWIS: Thanks, dad.

> [LEWIS goes inside.]

GRANDMA: You know nothing about Greek tragedy --

ERIC: It's what men learn from women.

[He's about to go inside.]

GRANDMA: Eric...[he turns back] Do you hear noises?

ERIC: Noises?

GRANDMA: Under the house.

ERIC: No. You must be going mad.

[He goes.]

SCENE ELEVEN

The RSL Club. Night. The sound of breaking glass. DULCIE, dressed as an angel, her wings covered in feathers from the pillows, enters, excited.

DULCIE: Come on.

LEWIS: [off] You broke the window.

[LEWIS, also dressed as an angel, enters.]

DULCIE: How else were we going to get in? They think RSL halls are sacred or something. They don't think that anyone'd have the guts to break in. [Finding some whisky.] Hey, what the doctor ordered. [She downs some and then gives it to LEWIS.] Drink. [LEWIS is reluctant.] It won't bite. [He downs a bit and splutters at its harshness.] Good, eh? [He goes to take off his wings.] What are you doing?

LEWIS: Taking them off.

DULCIE: Keep them on. All night. I made them for you.

LEWIS: The party's over.

DULCIE: It's just begun. [Taking a swig.] We won first prize. Told you we would. Are you going to thank me?

LEWIS: You forced me to wear them.

[She slaps him hard across the face.]

What's that for?

DULCIE: Can the Dutch girl do that?

[She laughs, excited. During the rest of the scene they take swigs of the whisky.]

We'll find some cards and nick them.

[She goes off in search of cards. A dog barks. LEWIS is nervous.]

DULCIE: It's only a dog.

LEWIS: Let's get going.

DULCIE: I want to steal some stuff.

LEWIS: What are you doing up there?

DULCIE: This is the billiard table that Stan uses.

LEWIS: Why are you doing that?

DULCIE: [laughing] Are they going to be surprised. Hey, fellas, what's this wet patch? Holy Hell, someone's pissed on it. It smells like girl's piss. Some girl has pissed on an RSL billiard table. [She laughs and laughs as she pisses.]

[Rumbling sounds of thunderstorm.]

LEWIS: Thunderstorm. Coming over the power station.

[He finds some cards.]

Hey, I got some cards.

[DULCIE enters and takes the cards from LEWIS and scatters them everywhere.]

I thought you wanted to steal them?

DULCIE: I want to make a mess of this place. We'll tear it up, piss and shit on it all and someone passing by will say tomorrow morning: I saw angels in the RSL hall. It was angels that destroyed it. [She grabs bottle and pours whisky down LEWIS' throat.] Nectar of the angels. [Touching his wings.] Aren't they beautiful? Angels hover in the air like dragonflies. Like this. Now I have no wings.

LEWIS: Yes, you do.

DULCIE: No, not yet. Angels have to think of them and then they imagine having them and there is a feeling, like it must be when boys get stiff, a growing from the shoulders. Two wings on either shoulders. But they don't look like wings at first, they look like buds, white buds. Then slowly, like a flower, they slowly open, breaking through the angels'

clothes. Real slow, unfolding like in dreamtime. And then
they open out, like my wings. They begin to float testing
new, unnamed muscles. Then they're like a bird flying, break
free of the ground. I begin to rise. Above you. Higher higher,
like a cloud, my body feels light as a cloud. I begin speaking
but my voice has changed, it's as loud as a scream, softer
than a whisper. I speak like an angel. My speech sounds like
this. [She presses her lips against his hands and says the
one phrase over and over.] I am saying something secret to
you in angel talk.

LEWIS: What are you saying?

    [She slaps him.]

DULCIE: You should know!

LEWIS: Stop hitting me.

DULCIE: I didn't. It was the angel. This is me, Dulcie, not the
angel.

    [She jumps on him.] Fight me. Fight me!

    [She is sitting on him.] Fight me!

LEWIS: I don't want to.

DULCIE: Wrestle me!

    [He shakes his head.]

    We'll play strip jack poker. I'll lose.

    [She takes a drink. He takes one.]

    Do you like me?

LEWIS: Yes.

    [He throws her off and takes another drink.]

DULCIE: Let's play war like we used to. I'll be the Nazi. You'll
be the American. [She spots a sash and grabs it.] You
capture me. Tie me up. [She grabs him.] I'm your prisoner,
Lewis. I'm a Nazi spy. Tie me here, around my hands.

LEWIS: It's a child's game.

    [He moves away to see the thunderstorm.]

    Lightning.

DULCIE: You hate me. What would you do if I fucked Brian?

    [LEWIS shrugs. Lightning strikes close by. DULCIE squeals
with delight.]

A storm! A storm!

[He goes to the radio.]

LEWIS: Some music.

[He turns it on only to get a news broadcast.]

RADIO: In other news today Prime Minister Menzies gave a stern warning to the Russians and threatened Australian retaliation if they bombed or invaded United States.

DULCIE: Turn it off. Music! Music!

[He finds another station. It is playing *Love is a many splendid thing*.]

Lewis!

[He thinks she is going to jump on him.]

I'm not Dulcie. I have taken over her body. I changed into a worm and crawled up inside her and took her over. I am an alien.

[Another bolt of lightning. She cries out.]

See me. See my true form!

[Quite tipsy by now, they both laugh.]

LEWIS: I have something to tell you. I'm an alien too.

DULCIE: Two in the same neighbourhood.

LEWIS: We're all aliens. We've taken over Earth.

[The music changes to the instrumental rock song *Telstar*. The two start running around the RSL Hall, excited, smashing things, throwing real plates and paper plates around.]

LEWIS: Flying saucers!

DULCIE: Flying saucers!

LEWIS: It's an attack of the UFOs.

DULCIE: Destroy earth!

LEWIS: Destroy! Destroy all earthly things!

DULCIE: We're conquering the world. We won!

LEWIS: We won!

DULCIE: The aliens are here!

[Thunder and lightning and music.]

BOTH: We're here! The aliens are here! The aliens are here!

ACT THREE

SCENE ONE

LEWIS is hosing the lawn. The JAPANESE WOMAN stands nearby, as if he is thinking of her. She giggles, he looks and smiles at her. There is a distant radio on and it is news about the crisis.

RADIO: The world has been holding its breath as the Cuban Crisis goes into its second week of stalemate. The United States and Russia are on war alert. As Senator Dobson said: 'If the situation were a clock, then it is reading two minutes to mid-night'.

[The news fades as LEWIS continues hosing, having paid no attention to it.]

NARRATOR: School had finished. It was the new year: January. The hot, northerly winds blew across the paddocks, scorching our skins and gardens. The storm on the night of the break-up party brought only electricity and my first hangover.

[PISANO running backwards and wearing only shorts and runners, enters.]

PISANO: Why are you watering the garden this time of morning, Lewis?

LEWIS: Water restrictions. Have to be done by nine.

PISANO: I don't have to abide by the law. Postmen are government men. Let your plants die. They're so scrawny, they're almost dead anyway. Merri Creek soil would have helped: it keeps the moisture. Least I know you mob aren't stealing my soil. Can't get over it. Thought I was seeing things. A bloody great big hole in my front garden. In the Harrison's, the Thompson's too. What low mongrel would steal your soil? I think it's the same people who are shooting cats. Maybe it's some sort of Satanic cult? Is your dad in?

LEWIS: [nervously] No. In town.

PISANO: I'll have to talk to him about his number. I know I go on about it, but it's important. Last night I was keeping watch for the bugger who's stealing my soil when I saw you and your dad out and about. What were you doing?

LEWIS: [lying] Looking for UFOs.

PISANO: UFOs? Your father always struck me as fairly level-headed.

LEWIS: Don't you believe in them?

PISANO: Flying saucers? My wife used to throw them at me. She's working in a Thai brothel. Thai men apparently like to lick a white woman's feet.

[He runs off on his delivery round.]

NARRATOR: Mr Pisano was right. It was pointless to water the garden. It wouldn't stop the grass from going brown and dying and those stunted plants, those English plants that every garden in those days had, unused to the heat, just gave up and shrivelled away. No one had natives in those days. January days were like a mirage.

[The JAPANESE WOMAN walks away as if vanishing into a mirage.]

Nothing was real, nothing truly happened. Dogs stayed under the house in the darkness and cool, panting, their tongues hanging out. The cracks in the soil grew larger, the concrete walls in our house grew so hot they were impossible to touch. There was nothing to relieve the heat. An Australian summer was longer and hotter then.

SCENE TWO

The kitchen. The radio report on the Cuban crisis which was distant, momentarily grows louder and then fades into the background. GRANDMA and NORMA, their nerves frayed by the heat, are talking, watching the budgie fly around the room.

GRANDMA: I don't want the window open.

NORMA: It's boiling in here.

GRANDMA: Sam needs to be free. He needs to have his exercise.

NORMA: I don't want him to, he shits everywhere.

GRANDMA: He's a budgie. He needs to fly.

NORMA: Give him his freedom then, let him fly out the window.

GRANDMA: He'll be killed by a eagle. They love budgies.

NORMA: He won't be killed by an eagle. I'll wring his bloody neck.

　　　　[BEV walks through the kitchen.]

NORMA: Where are you going to, miss?

BEV: A walk. To see June.

NORMA: What about the washing?

BEV: When I come back.

　　　　[Out she goes.]

NORMA: What's getting into her?

GRANDMA: Boys.

NORMA: If I can turn off the radio, he can continue to fly around.

GRANDMA: It's the news. The news about the world. [Realising her part in the deal.] All right.

　　　　[NORMA goes and turns off the radio as LEWIS enters.]

NORMA: Finished watering?

LEWIS: Yeh.

NORMA: [correcting him] Yes.

LEWIS: Yes.

NORMA: I want you to do some weeding.

GRANDMA: Let the poor boy alone.

NORMA: It's part of his punishment. He taught that Dutch girl those filthy words. I was never so ashamed as when the headmaster tried to tell me what he'd taught her. He had to write them out on a piece of paper. Where did he learn them?

GRANDMA: Here. On this housing estate, of course,

NORMA: Then coming home roaring drunk from the break-up party.

GRANDMA: Memory is all we've got.

NORMA: What?

GRANDMA: Memory. Without memory we are nothing. I'm losing mine.

NORMA: It's the heat. I'll open the window.

GRANDMA: I want Sam to fly.

[ERIC enters, smiling, confident.]

NORMA: How did it go?

ERIC: I'm just in the door.

GRANDMA: He didn't get the job.

ERIC: What makes you think that?

GRANDMA: You're so happy.

NORMA: Mum!

GRANDMA: My bludging son-in-law.

NORMA: You've been to the pub.

ERIC: You jump on a man. [To LEWIS] More Greek tragedy.

NORMA: We were better off when you were not here.

ERIC: Give a man a break. I've been back a month. The factories are closed down over the Christmas break.

NORMA: You could get a job if you really wanted to.

GRANDMA: Men only bring chaos into the home. Sam loves flying.

[Watching him dive bombing.]

Whish! Whish! Look at him go!

NORMA: Why did I marry you?

[She rushes out, upset.]

ERIC: [smiling, to LEWIS] What would happen if a man rushed out, crying all the time. Nothing would get done. No planes would have been invented. No telephones, gramophones, electric lights, cars, no tunnels dug. Twinkle, twinkle little star, three days and there you are. [Sotto voce.] Tonight. [He goes.]

LEWIS: Mr Pisano, dad!

> [But his father doesn't hear. The bird circles overhead. They both watch it.]

GRANDMA: Ladybird, ladybird, fly away home.

> [She faints.]

LEWIS: [hurrying to her] Grandma, what's the matter? Wake up.Grandma...[She wakes.]

GRANDMA: What am I doing here? Why's the ceiling so far away?

LEWIS: You fainted.

GRANDMA: I did no such thing.

LEWIS: You said 'ladybird, ladybird' and fainted.

GRANDMA: You're talking shit. Pure shit. [Even she is surprised at what she has said. She gets to her feet with LEWIS' help.] Excuse my French. I did not faint. Did I?

> [He shakes his head, agreeing with her.]

Oops, sorry, Sam's pooped in your hair. Naughty, Sam. Naughty.

SCENE THREE

Near the power station. PISANO is walking quickly carrying a large paint can and a paint brush. DULCIE watches him in the darkness. She is dressed like a boy.

DULCIE: Hello, Mr Pisano.

PISANO: [shocked] Dulcie.

DULCIE: What are you doing?

PISANO: Just out and about. Night time on the estate is becoming busier than the day. You running away?

DULCIE: I'm waiting for Lewis.

PISANO: Your father's not selling stolen soil, is he?

DULCIE: Soil?

PISANO: Never mind. I can imagine him stealing nightsoil

but never real soil.

[He goes. DULCIE has been waiting for LEWIS for some time and is growing impatient. She sees him approaching and she drops to the ground pretending to be praying.]

DULCIE: Allah, be praised. Allah, be praised. [Without looking up.] You're late.

LEWIS: Dad's preparing a birthday present for mum, he wanted me to help.

DULCIE: Allah, be praised.

LEWIS: East is that way.

DULCIE: [irritated] I'm not an orthodox Moslem, right?

LEWIS: [noticing she is dressed like a boy] Why are you dressed like that?

DULCIE: What's the matter with it?

LEWIS: Stupid, that's all.

DULCIE: You want to break into the RSL hall again? [LEWIS shakes his head.] Dad keeps on talking about 'Who desecrated the RSL? When I catch them I'm going to cut off their balls'. Better watch out, Lewis. [LEWIS moves on] Where you going?

LEWIS: Over here. So I can see the power lines. They'll come along tracking the power lines.

DULCIE: Do you know what I think? I think life is only a dream. [LEWIS laughs.] We're the dream of a mentally ill angel.

LEWIS: We're the dream of an alien who is imagining what life must be like on that distant planet called Earth.

[She laughs, then goes serious.]

DULCIE: Maybe aliens have taken over someone like Mr Pisano? It's possible, isn't it? He's doing his rounds but no one is getting mail.

LEWIS: He's a bit worried. Apparently Thai men are licking his wife's feet.

DULCIE: That American who went to Venus, he said there were no males or females. That means they don't put their cocks up women. They don't hurt them.

LEWIS: [seeing something] Get down.

DULCIE: What is it?

LEWIS: Down by the creek. Two people.

DULCIE: We're doing nothing wrong.

LEWIS: They might be guards from the power station.

[DULCIE laughs.]

What's wrong with you?

DULCIE: It's your sister Bev. She's with Brian.

LEWIS: [incredulously] It isn't.

DULCIE: It is.

LEWIS: She hates him. She hit him with a cricket bat.

DULCIE: He probably liked it.

LEWIS: You're stupid sometimes. [He stands up.] They've gone.

DULCIE: In the creek doing it.

LEWIS: It wasn't them.

[Pause.]

DULCIE: You liked me dressed as a boy?

LEWIS: I don't care how you're dressed.

DULCIE: You like my hair up?

LEWIS: I just want to look for UFOs. [Knowing he had better answer.]

Down.

DULCIE: [unpinning it] Like this. [It falls down. LEWIS looks at it dispassionately.] You really prefer boys, don't you?

LEWIS: Just let me look for UFOs!

DULCIE: Are you jealous that Brian is with your sister?

LEWIS: He's not with my sister.

DULCIE: Pretend I'm a boy.

LEWIS: Leave me alone.

DULCIE: I'll lick your feet like a Thai man.

LEWIS: Just leave me alone. Go and fuck Brian.

DULCIE: Can't, your sister's got in before me. [She starts to go, then stops, yelling back] You're a child. [Shouting out as she goes] Snake! Snake!

NARRATOR: [watching LEWIS] Doesn't make sense, does it? [LEWIS shakes his head.]
There must be some reason why people behave the way they do.
[LEWIS spins around slowly, staring at the sky.]
What are you thinking?

LEWIS: There is another world out there where everything makes sense. There was a man who was taken to Mars. The canals were perfect, yet everything was a mirror reflection of earth. Left was right, right was left. People didn't hurt one another. Everything that was bad and stupid in our world was perfect on Mars. Dreams were reality, reality was a dream. When it was sunny the Martians put up their umbrellas – and fold them up when it's raining. [He stops spinning.] The prickles are getting into my shoes.
[LEWIS hears a noise and turns around to see BEV and BRIAN who are amused to have seen LEWIS spinning around talking to himself.]

BRIAN: Talking to yourself, spinning around and around, you're getting weird, Lewis.

LEWIS: What were you doing with my sister?

BRIAN: It's none of your business.

LEWIS: Just piss off. I don't want you anywhere near here.

BEV: You can't push him around.

LEWIS: Yes, I can.

BEV: He's my friend.

LEWIS: You're my sister. I know what he thinks about girls. I know what he wants.

BEV: So what? What about you and Dulcie?

LEWIS: I don't do anything like that with her.

BRIAN: Well, from what I've heard, you're the only one who doesn't.
[LEWIS punches him to the ground.]

LEWIS: Don't ever touch her!

BRIAN: [surprised at the attack, now angry] I'm going to belt the shit out of you.

BEV: [to BRIAN] Don't. Go home, I'll deal with him.

LEWIS: Deal with me?

BEV: [to BRIAN] Home! I'll see you tomorrow.

BRIAN: [to LEWIS] If she wasn't your sister, I'd fuckin' flatten you. I'll remember that punch. Keep it up here. I've got a memory like an elephant. Like me dad.

[He goes. Pause.]

BEV: You think other people are looney, but wake up to yourself, Lewis. All you know and care about are flying saucers and they're not real. They don't exist. I'm going to see Brian and I don't care what you think. You're a child.

[Silence.]

You going to tell mum about me and Brian?

[He shakes his head.]

Thank you. [A beat.] You're all right for a brother.

[She kisses him on the cheek.]

LEWIS: Why did you hit Brian on the head with the cricket bat.

BEV: Because I love him. It was the only way to get his attention.

[She goes.]

NARRATOR: It was some night. The next morning the police were called. During the night huge house numbers had been painted on every front door. Mr Pisano confessed, telling the police he had had to resort to drastic measures, or what he called 'drastic messages'. No one knew what it was like having to search for house numbers every day. And no one knew what it was like to be humiliated by your wife working in a Thai brothel. [LEWIS and ERIC enter with spade and wheelbarrow.] It was thought he had been under great stress because of his wife, so he wasn't charged. The post office wanted to put him on sick leave but he would hear nothing of that. 'The round is my way back to health', he told them.

LEWIS: [spotting postman] Pisano!

ERIC: Quick, behind that bush!

[ERIC throws the spade in the wheelbarrow and LEWIS wheels it off into the darkness as a jogging PISANO, wearing proper postman's clothes enters.]

PISANO: UFO spotting?

ERIC: [confused, agrees] Yes. Good night for it.

PISANO: Really? There seems to be lots of clouds.

ERIC: Late delivering your mail. Bit behind are you?

PISANO: The heat was getting to me so I decided to take advantage of the night. Cooler, then. Time to think. Think deeply.

ERIC: We don't seem to be getting as much mail as we used to.

PISANO: You don't seriously want more bills do you? The only one I'm not delivering mail to is that Johnson fellow. Tried to deliver a registered letter yesterday and he pointed a rifle at me. That's what happens when you marry a dago.

[He laughs and heads off.]

ERIC: [to himself]   Twinkle, twinkle, little star

                        One more night and there you are.

[LEWIS comes out of hiding.]

LEWIS: Perhaps we've got enough soil.

ERIC: Stop being a chicken. Even after tonight we might not have enough.

LEWIS: What'll we do then?

ERIC: Take some soil from under the house itself. Now, where to tonight?

ERIC: Pisano's.

LEWIS: He's already suspicious.

ERIC: He's still got the rest of his round to do.

[Off they go, ERIC first, followed by a reluctant LEWIS.]

SCENE FOUR

Backyard. LEWIS' house. Late afternoon. BEV leading NORMA, who is wearing a blindfold, out into the backyard.

NORMA: But why am I blindfolded?

BEV: A surprise.

NORMA: I feel lost.

BEV: You're supposed to.

> [LEWIS is raking the last of the soil on the back lawn. ERIC is impatient for LEWIS to finish.]

ERIC: Hurry, Lewis.

BEV: Dad and Lewis have a surprise for you.

> [LEWIS hurries off with his barrow and rake. ERIC indicates where BEV should take NORMA.]

This way, mum.

NORMA: How long do I keep this on?

BEV: Not long now.

> [GRANDMA comes out as ERIC indicates that BEV should spin NORMA.]

NORMA: What are you doing?

BEV: It's part of the surprise.

NORMA: I'm getting giddy.

BEV: Good.

> [LEWIS comes outside and BEV stops spinning her mother.]

NORMA: The world is turning.

BEV: It'll stop in a moment.

> [She takes off the blindfold. NORMA is stunned at what she sees.]

Has it stopped?

ERIC: Like a billiard table, isn't it?

NORMA: You've levelled the lawn.

ERIC: Spirit levelled.

NORMA: You did it.

ERIC: Me and Lewis.

NORMA: It's wonderful. [She kisses LEWIS, then ERIC.] Thank you. Both of you.

[She admires the backyard.]

GRANDMA: First decent thing you've ever done, Eric.

ERIC: [sarcastically] Thank you, mum.

NORMA: Where did you get the soil?

ERIC: Manna from the sky. A miracle.

NORMA: You bought it?

ERIC: It was free.

NORMA: Free?

ERIC: You can grow anything on it. It's the best soil. Flower beds there. Vegetable garden down the back. Willow trees along the side, like you get along the Murray.

NORMA: It's very black.

ERIC: Rich Merri Creek soil.

NORMA: Merri Creek?

ERIC: Only the best for you.

[Her suspicions are growing.]

NORMA: Where did you keep it?

ERIC: Keep what?

NORMA: The soil. The stolen soil.

ERIC: What are you on about?

NORMA: I am not entirely stupid. Lewis, did you steal the soil?

[LEWIS looks to his father for some guidance.]

ERIC: [to LEWIS] Women always find it difficult to accept presents.

NORMA: It was you. You stole the soil from people's gardens!

ERIC: It's not as if we dug great big bloody quarries in every front yard. A tiny bit from here, a little from there, that's all, they hardly missed it!

[Silence.]

NORMA: I want you to return it.

ERIC: You must be mad. The yard is level. Fertile.

NORMA: Return the soil.

[Pause.]

Today!
>   [Pause.]
ERIC: How about tonight. It's nightsoil. We stole it at night.
>   [Pause.]
NORMA: Tonight then.
GRANDMA: You couldn't even marry a real criminal.
NORMA: Any more out of you and Sam will never shit in anyone's hair again.
>   [She goes inside.]
ERIC: [to LEWIS] Once she's calmed down, she'll change her mind. She'll see the benefits of what we've done.

SCENE FIVE

NARRATOR: We returned the soil. It took us a week. We filled the holes we had dug and if they had been filled in the meantime we deposited the soil near the front doors so, dad said, 'the spastics could see that their soil had been returned'. Mum and Dad didn't say another word to each other. We children passed on their messages.
>   [Lights up on NORMA laying out playing cards to tell her fortune. She is in the house. Outside, ERIC is in the backyard.]
ERIC: [to himself.] It could have been the most perfect backyard on the whole estate. [A beat.] Greek tragedy. That's what it is. [He starts singing the song Carrickfergus.]

> I wished I had you in Carrickfergus
> Only for nights in Ballygrand
> I would swim over the deepest ocean
> The deepest ocean to be by your side.

>   [BEV comes into the house prepared to go out for the night.]
BEV: I'm off.
NORMA: Too much make up, darling.

BEV: But does it look good?

NORMA: Very pretty.

BEV: Like you when you were young?

NORMA: Like me when I was young.

[NORMA goes back to playing cards.]

ERIC: But the sea is wide and I can't swim over
and neither have I wings to fly
I wish I could find me a handy boatman
To ferry me over to my love and die.

BEV: You reading the cards?

NORMA: Seeing the future.

BEV: Is it good?

NORMA: I don't know. I haven't read them, all yet. You have to take them in sequence.

BEV: Dad's out in the backyard singing.

NORMA: He used to always sing that song when he said goodbye to me when he left me at night.

BEV: Will you read my future soon?

NORMA: There's no need. You've got a wonderful one. Do be careful with the boys.

BEV: Were you careful with dad?

NORMA: He was my first and only boyfriend. I was very naive. [Kisses her goodnight.] Be home before twelve.

BEV: Yes.

[She goes.]

ERIC: And in Kilkenny it is reported
on Marble as black as ink
with gold and silver I did support her
but I'll sing no more until I get a drink.

[NORMA is looking at her future when GRANDMA screams and hurries in.]

GRANDMA: [coming in] Sam! Sam!

NORMA: What's the matter.

GRANDMA: Someone's cut off Sam's head. It's in the seed tray.

NORMA: You sure.

GRANDMA: It's in the seed tray. Someone has murdered my
    Sam.

NORMA: No one's murdered your budgie.

GRANDMA: Someone has murdered him!

NORMA: [finding herself laughing] They haven't.

GRANDMA: You have!

NORMA: I haven't!

GRANDMA: You're laughing!

NORMA: It's only a budgie.

GRANDMA: You murdered him!

NORMA: I didn't.

    [GRANDMA storms out.]

  Mum!

    [But she's gone. NORMA shakes her head and laughs at
    the notion of the decapitated budgie.]

ERIC: So I'll spend my days in endless roving
                     soft is the grass and my bed is free
                     Oh to be home now in Carrickfergus
                     on the long road down to the salty sea

NARRATOR: He always appeared singing *It's all in the game* and
left singing *Carrickfergus*. He was possessed by distance.
Marriage and children couldn't compete with that. [A beat.]
He went that summer night saying he was going to see a
friend. As we used to say 'He went walkabout'. We got a
postcard from Darwin, saying he would be coming back once
he made money working a mine. It was the last time I saw
him. He never returned.

    [To ERIC.] Where did you go after that?

ERIC: Wherever you imagined I did. I went searching for
Lasseter's Reef, marlin fishing off Cape York, kangaroo
shooting in Back of Bourke, became a stock car driver, drove
motorbikes through a wall of fire, lived underground for
years mining opals.

                  I'm drunk today and I'm rarely sober
                  A handsome rover from town to town.

NARRATOR: We missed him.

ERIC: Oh, but I am sick now and my days are
                    numbered
                    Come all ye young men and lay me
                    down.

NARRATOR: We forgave him. But then, we forgive fathers
everything.

[ERIC vanishes.]

I returned to my world of women. I began to lose interest in
UFOs, wondering if I would ever see one again.

SCENE SIX

The crossroads. Night. Beatrice is waiting there with her snake
stick. She smiles at the NARRATOR.

BEATRICE: Bugger. Fuck. Piss. Shit.

NARRATOR: I still went walking at night. Anything to help my
asthma. Sometimes I came across the Dutch girl walking in
the paddocks. I used to wonder if she was thinking of home,
back in her world of green grass, dykes and wooden clogs.
I knew that she knew she swearing when the teacher asked
her what words she had learnt in Australia.

BEATRICE: Shit. Fuck. Bugger. Piss.

NARRATOR: [waving] Hello.

BEATRICE: Hello, Lewis. Shit. Bugger. Piss. Fuck.

NARRATOR: You knew what you were saying, didn't you?

[She smiles and turns away poking a hole for snakes.]

BEATRICE: Snake! Snake!

NARRATOR: I hadn't seen Dulcie for a week and I found I was
missing her more than I thought I would have. I went to her
house to see if she wanted to come out in the paddocks with
me. It was late at night. There was a light on in her room. I
peeked through a crack in the curtain.

[Lights come up on NARRATOR and LEWIS remembering this moment. It is a harsh, vivid memory: MR IRVIN is sitting on a chair, wearing a dressing gown and nothing else underneath. DULCIE is on his knee. She is sullen as he touches her breasts, and kisses her ear. He grabs her hand and puts it on his groin. Not looking at the scene, LEWIS closes his eyes at the memory of it.]

NARRATOR: What did you see?

LEWIS: Nothing.

NARRATOR: Open your eyes!

[LEWIS opens his eyes, staring ahead as if he can see the scene etched vividly on his mind.]

What do you see?

LEWIS: She is on his lap.

NARRATOR: What is Mr Irvin doing?

LEWIS: Nothing.

[Pause.]

NARRATOR: What is she doing?

LEWIS: She's touching him. Then he got her to touch his penis.

NARRATOR: Is she enjoying it?

LEWIS: No.

NARRATOR: Maybe he's possessed by aliens?

[Pause.]

LEWIS: No. He just wants her. He doesn't care if she doesn't want him. I've always thought he was a shit of a human being, now I know.

[He takes out his spray as he finds it hard to breathe. Pause, then the scene fades.]

I just don't want to think about it any more. Ever.

SCENE SEVEN

The backyard. Night. GRANDMA is listening to a transistor. The news is good.

RADIO: This afternoon, Australian time, the Russian government backed down from its previous stance and just a few minutes before the United States deadline, agreed to remove its missiles from Cuba. The reaction, worldwide, has been one of relief.

[GRANDMA throws the transistor away into the darkness. It breaks and stops.]

GRANDMA: Relief...for how long. Boys being boys...[She stares at the backyard.] Looks like a quarry.

[LEWIS enters, preoccupied by what he has seen.]

Your mother was too honest. The backyard's so uneven now that you could break your ankle. Out UFO spotting?

LEWIS: Just walking. Helps my asthma.

GRANDMA: It's the pollen blown by the northerlies. You'll grow out of it when you're older. Did you see any flying saucers?

LEWIS: No. Just Brian's dad down at the rifle range. He said he was going to start practising shooting at night.

[A loud noise is heard.]

GRANDMA: What was that?

LEWIS: Sounded like a gun. Must be Brian's dad.

GRANDMA: A car backfiring. Where was I? Age. Growing old. [A beat.] You must kill me when I get old. Your grandfather was older than me and I had to clean him. Dribbles down his mouth. Earwax. Sleepdust. Urine. Shit. His body was out of control. Vomit. Lots of vomit. Diarrhoea. That's old age. Put a pillow over my face; I won't struggle. No one will know you've done it. Not those new fangled sponge ones. Make sure the pillow's filled with feathers. I'll plug up all my holes so you won't have to clean up the shit and blood. Excuse my French.

[Pause.]

I wish I could sleep. I lay awake on my couch listening, not to the voices, which have thankfully gone, but to the house cracking. Don't ever, ever believe any person when they say they're enjoying their old age.

[She goes inside. As night turns to day, LEWIS practises his bowling.]

NARRATOR: Grandma gave up her obsession with me suffocating her when she had heard how Brian's father had shot himself down at the rifle range.

LEWIS: [to himself as he practises] Maybe he did it there so his wife didn't have to clean the ceiling.

NARRATOR: Brian didn't say much about it. He kept to himself. Lost interest in girls and stayed at home all night watching television. Bev quickly got another boyfriend. 'Brian's no fun any more', she said. No one knew why his father had killed himself. He left no note.

[NORMA enters with MRS IRVIN.]

NORMA: Lewis, Mrs Irvin would like a word with you.

[Pause.]

MRS IRVIN: I want you to tell me the truth about you and Dulcie.

[A beat.]

She's been telling lies. I want the truth. Will you do that?

LEWIS: Yes.

[She hands him the clear plastic box, the size of a matchbox that contains the sliver of St Thomas's bone.]

MRS IRVIN: Kiss the bone and promise to tell the truth.

LEWIS: [kissing the bone] I promise to tell the truth.

[He gives back the box.]

MRS IRVIN: Did you and Dulcie fornicate?

[Momentarily confused by the word he looks to his mother.]

Did you?

LEWIS: [realising] Ah, fornicate?

MRS IRVIN: Yes.

LEWIS: No.

MRS IRVIN: Dulcie's been telling lies.

NORMA: About she and Lewis?

MRS IRVIN: About she and Stan.

[A beat.]

This morning the police came and took him away because of her lies.

NORMA: Took him away.

MRS IRVIN: I should have put her away at birth, but I kept her. She was born in lies and so I've reaped what I have sown. I lied about her father. He wasn't Basque. Just an Aborigine I met up near Townsville. Blood never lies. Once a gin, always a gin. This time he'll be in jail for years because of her. There'll be no money and the man I love will be in jail for years. [to LEWIS] Before the eyes of God, you didn't fornicate?

LEWIS: No.

[A beat.]

MRS IRVIN: I'm off to visit him now. We can't afford the bail, so he'll have to stay there until the court case.

NORMA: What about Dulcie?

MRS IRVIN: I'm doing what I should have done years ago. She's going to a Girls' Home. Her mind should be thoroughly washed out. Stan is not an animal. [To LEWIS] Thank you for telling the truth. Good day.

[She goes.]

NORMA: You did tell the truth?

LEWIS: Yes.

NORMA: But you are keen on Dulcie?

[He shrugs.]

SCENE EIGHT

The crossroads. Night.

NARRATOR: The more I thought about Dulcie and her stepfather, the more agitated I became.

[LEWIS comes on breathing with effort because of his asthma.]

It's hard to breathe, isn't it?

  [LEWIS nods.]

What are you doing here at the crossroads. Why aren't you down near the power station?

LEWIS: I just want to walk. Breathe. Catch my breath.

  [DULCIE enters wearing her angel outfit.]

DULCIE: I knew you'd be here.

  [Pause.]

I'm not going to sleep tonight. I'm going to be wide awake when they come and get me tomorrow morning.

  [Pause.]

You don't care about me. You only care about your flying saucers.

LEWIS: I'm not looking for them. I'm just trying to breathe.

  [DULCIE shows him a small object.]

What's that?

DULCIE: Mum's bone of St Thomas. I substituted it with a piece of rabbit bone. [She throws the bone far away and laughs.] Now she can pray to a rabbit! [They both laugh.]...Remember when we were going to be acrobats? We always kept our things ready in a bag, ready to run away. [A beat.] Let's run away. [He shakes his head.] You're a coward.

LEWIS: Where do you want to run?

DULCIE: Anywhere?

LEWIS: You have to know where you're running.

DULCIE: You don't care a fig for me. [A beat.] There's no point in watching the skies. The aliens are here. They live in people. They change them. Make them do things that are cruel. Stan is possessed by aliens. So is your father. They're infected.

LEWIS: There are no aliens. No flying saucers.

DULCIE: How come they're infected then? [She flings off her wings and rushes at him.] Geronimo! [She wrestles him.]

LEWIS: Don't. Don't! Get off.

DULCIE: No.

[Suddenly he goes into a rage, a fury of anger and he starts to wrestle and hit her.]

DULCIE: Lewis don't! Don't hurt me!

LEWIS: I hate you! I hate you!

[He straddles her, sitting on top of her. Silence. They breathe heavily with the effort of fighting.]

Why do you make me hit you?

[Pause.]

DULCIE: I want you to react.

[Pause.]

You do hate me then?

LEWIS: I don't hate you.

DULCIE: Why did you say it then?

LEWIS: Same reason my sister hit Brian on the head with the cricket bat, I guess.

[Pause.]

DULCIE: [angrily] Get off me!

LEWIS: No!

DULCIE: I'll scream.

[He kisses her gently on the lips. Pause.]

DULCIE: Why did you do that?

LEWIS: So I wouldn't hit you with a cricket bat.

DULCIE: You're weird.

LEWIS: [getting off her] I don't know why I do anything. [He is kneeling looking at the sky.] Maybe we don't see UFOs any more because they took one look at humans and fled back to their own planet.

[DULCIE laughs. She crawls over to him putting on her wings again.]

DULCIE: [from behind him] I'm your guardian angel. What present would you like? Tell me and I'll give it to you.

LEWIS: [getting in the spirit of things] New boots. Cowboy boots. Made of rattlesnake. [The NARRATOR, who is watching this, and who is wearing rattlesnake boots, smiles. She can move her wings, when she moves her shoulders. She comes around to face LEWIS.]

DULCIE: Done! [A beat.] Angels do not talk about their feelings. But their wings talk. If they move gently like this they are amused by something a human has done. Kiss me.

[He kisses her lightly on the lips. She gently ruffles her wings.]

See.

[Moves them more strongly.]

I am pleased that humans believe in me.

[Then broadly, but slowly and gracefully.]

This is almost like flying, but it isn't. I am in ecstasy and although a human can't see me, the one who believes in me can feel the breeze from my beating wings. Close your eyes. [He closes his eyes.] Can you feel the breeze? [He nods.] It's called an angel's breath. I am in ecstasy.

[She kisses him passionately. He jumps away, not wanting to let himself go with her.]

DULCIE: What is it?

LEWIS: Nothing.

DULCIE: Make love to me.

LEWIS: I don't want to.

DULCIE: You do.

[Pause.]

Why not?

[Silence. She is devastated at his rejection.]

NARRATOR: Go back. [LEWIS stops.] Go back to her. Turn around and go back. [LEWIS turns and faces her.] Go on, walk back to her. [He walks back to her and stands looking down at her. Silence.]

DULCIE: Do you like me?

NARRATOR: Answer her.

LEWIS: Yes.

DULCIE: Very much?

LEWIS: Very much.

NARRATOR: Get down on the ground. [LEWIS joins her on the ground.] Grab her. And kiss her. [LEWIS does as he's told] Now do what she wants and you want to do.

[They lie down together, kissing. Pause.]

We made love in the paddocks and then we lay down together, not saying anything, just listening to the hum of the power station and the telephone lines singing. We stayed out until dawn and watched the sun rise.

[LEWIS stands up and holds out his hand. DULCIE grabs it and he pulls her up.]

DULCIE: Will you visit me in the home?

LEWIS: Yes.

DULCIE: I have to stay there until I'm sixteen and then we'll run away together.

LEWIS: Yes. To Japan. I'll buy you a kimono.

DULCIE: This is the happiest day of my life.

LEWIS: Mine too.

[She presses her lips against his hand and says something.]

DULCIE: Do you understand?

LEWIS: No.

DULCIE: I wish you had.

LEWIS: Do it again.

DULCIE: Too late! [A sudden jump to wild excitement.] Let's set fire to the paddocks. Like Brian's father used to do. Imagine that he was practising shooting himself. [Laughing.] So he wouldn't miss! Do you want to burn them. Burn everything?

[LEWIS falls to the ground and starts praying.]

LEWIS: Allah, be praised.

[DULCIE joins him.]

BOTH: [shouting] Allah, be praised! Allah, be praised!

[Then laughing they get up and kiss.]

NARRATOR: We set fire to the paddocks. They burnt quickly. They were bone dry. We watched until it was out of control, then I said goodbye to her and watched her crawl back inside her window.

[DULCIE goes.]

The hot northerly wind fanned the fire and it raced across the paddocks, devouring, the grass and the scotch thistles.

[Lights come up on NORMA, BEV, GRANDMA, the JAPANESE WOMAN, MRS IRVIN watching the fire coming closer. LEWIS arrives home.]

The fire rushed towards Singapore Street.

BEV: I saw Mr Pisano running towards the fire. He was throwing bags of mail into it.

NORMA: At least we've got an excuse not to pay the bills.

[Lights up on DULCIE on her swing.]

DULCIE: [swinging back and forth] An angel is passing. He's stopping, and he is listening to us and we explain the beauty and suffering of our world, but we can't explain it properly.

NARRATOR: [As the only one watching her.] I never visited her in the Home. Never saw her again.

[A beat.]

What happened to you?

Where did you go?

DULCIE: I don't know, because you don't know.

BEV: Mr Pisano's taking off his clothes!

GRANDMA: Charming. Double charming.

BEV: He's dancing.

MRS IRVIN: It's getting closer. This time it won't stop.

DULCIE: We only mumble, stumble, not make sense. The angel understands though. Then he presses his lips against my hand.

NARRATOR: I realised that there were no aliens or flying saucers. People are just people.

NORMA: Turn on the hose, it's coming.

NARRATOR: It was a summer like no other.

BEV: Maybe he's celebrating the Russians giving in?

NARRATOR: I did love her, though I didn't understand this until years later when I saw her in the face of my lovers and wished they were her.

DULCIE: He says a word into my hand. What is that word, Lewis?

NARRATOR: I realised what the word was later. Years later. Too late.

BEV: [excited, pleased] It's coming. It's coming!

LEWIS: [excited too] It's gonna jump the street!

> [No one attempts to run away. NORMA has the hose ready but every one is staring at the approaching fire as if mesmerised.]

NARRATOR: Eventually Lewis and I merged. To become me, because of him.

DULCIE: [swinging back and forth] Catch me! Catch me, Lewis.

> [Tableau of everyone watching the fire, except for DULCIE, in her own reverie, swinging back and forth.]

NARRATOR: The fire came closer and closer, burning so brightly that the flames were reflected on our windows and it was like our house was on fire. But, as usual, no matter how much we wanted it to cross the street, it never did.

THE END

POSTSCRIPT

Any production of *Summer of the Aliens* is to exclude Scene 6, Act One.

Louis Nowra
December 1993